Weary, Burdened
& Burned Out

Weary Burdened & Burned Out

Finding Green Pastures for Pastors, Chaplains, and Leaders Caught on the Ministry Treadmill

Christopher Bassett, D. Min.
Pastor & Chaplain

Tampa, Florida

WEARY, BURDENED & BURNED OUT

Finding Green Pastures for Pastors, Chaplains, and Leaders Caught on the Ministry Treadmill

Printed in the USA

ISBN (print): 979-8-9869064-0-9

ISBN (EPUB): 979-8-9869064-1-6

Library of Congress Control Number (LCCN): 2022916351

Edited by Wendy K. Walters

Prepared for Publication by www.palmtreeproductions.com

Published by 4th Dimension Ministries, Tampa, FL

To contact the author: www.4thDimensionMinistries.org

DEDICATION

This is dedicated to my children, who have constantly encouraged me to write a book.

And to my loving wife, Cheri, who stood by me through the best and the worst that ministry has to offer, patiently waiting for me to see—despite my constant dismissals of her warnings that I was burning out—that ministry did not have to be a treadmill experience.

"COME TO ME, ALL WHO LABOR
AND ARE HEAVY LADEN, AND I WILL
GIVE YOU REST. TAKE MY YOKE
UPON YOU, AND LEARN FROM ME,
FOR I AM GENTLE AND LOWLY IN
HEART, AND YOU WILL FIND REST
FOR YOUR SOULS. FOR MY YOKE IS
EASY, AND MY BURDEN IS LIGHT."

MATTHEW 11:28-30, ESV

PRAISE FOR WEARY, BURDENED & BURNED OUT

I appreciate greatly the way in which Dr. Bassett has used my measure in his work. I set out to gather research data. He has set out to bring benefit from the research for serving ministers. This seems to me to be a good partnership. On the way, Chris has gathered and skillfully used the qualitative data to illuminate and properly critique the quantitative research. Well done! I hope Chris will find ways to bring these insights into the academic literature, as well as through his book.

LESLIE FRANCIS, M.A., Ph.D., M.Th. B.D., Sc.D., D.Div., D.Litt.
Professor of Religions and Education, Religions and Education Research Unit, The University of Warwick

Weary, Burdened & Burned Out by Christopher Bassett is masterfully written, and it immediately apprehends the heart. As someone who has been in ministry for over 35 years, I have witnessed friends in the service of God weary and burned out, resulting in losing their way. It was heartbreaking to watch as the loss included their ministry and marriage. Chris' sound biblical approach is fueled with transparent humility, love, grace, and compassion as he bares his soul by sharing his personal journey. More than a good book, this is needed medicine for those who are serving (or have served) God and find themselves burned out. It will help bring healing as well as act as a spiritual serum to prevent others from falling into this trap of the enemy. This book is not only for pastors and ministers but also for the Body of Christ as a whole. It will give church family members greater insight into what their leaders face to better love and support them.

DON STURIANO
Sr. Leader of Kingdom Life Christian Church in Bradenton, Florida

While burnout occurs in every occupation, statistics show that caregivers suffer burnout at a much higher rate. In this thought-provoking and timely book, Dr. Bassett shares his own struggle along with practical tools and resources for dealing with burnout. This inspiring work will help students and caregivers in all occupations to discover hope and find sources of resilience. If you read it with an open heart and mind, it just might change your life.

DR. BRIAN BOHLMAN, B.C.C.
Founder, Chaplain Training Academy

Occasionally you come across a book that reads your mail. After fifty-plus years in ministry and nine years as a volunteer First Responder Chaplain, this book did just that. Denial is one of the worst enemies of ministers. Because we accept that we are called by God, we refuse to believe we can fail. We realize too late that we can. I now know burnout has been a personal struggle I have tried to ignore. I no longer can.

Dr. Bassett's book has opened a door that I am confident will cause me to lay aside my superman complex and seek help for greater wholeness. This book will be a life-changing perspective for any minister, chaplain, or pastor who has lived and served in the trenches of ministry.

PHILIP R. BYLER, D.R.E., D.Div.
Pastor Emeritus of Trinity Church of McCaysville, GA

Weary, Burdened & Burned Out maintains the academic credibility of a doctoral thesis while artfully adjusting its language to be accessible and inviting to all. Filled with interviews, thought-provoking questions, and personal anecdotes, this book will challenge you to assess your level of emotional exhaustion and degree of personal satisfaction in ministry and take steps to address or prevent ministry burnout. Bassett's invitation to leave the treadmill and walk in the pasturelands is refreshing to the soul.

WENDY K. WALTERS
Editor, Author, Ghostwriter, Seventh Generation Minister

CONTENTS

INTRODUCTION

*"Give instruction to a wise person and he will
become still wiser; Teach a righteous person
and he will increase his insight."* [1]

I see you. Disappointed. Discouraged. Isolated. Dealing with betrayal. Feeling bitter. Struggling to remember the passion that first led you into ministry. You wonder if it is worth your time and money to read a book on ministry burnout. Will it help? Can anything help?

Or maybe you are in denial. Perhaps you are finding lots of other reasons that could explain why you have been feeling "off" or "not yourself." Maybe the subject of ministry burnout is a scary one for you. Perhaps it's a topic you want to avoid altogether.

I encourage you to think again.

Burnout can be devastating—*or* it can be instructional. No one escapes its symptoms who ventures great things in their lives. Those who do not heed its warning signs will ultimately succumb to its effects. Whether you recognize that you are approaching burnout, have reached burnout, or simply want to learn how to establish healthy life habits to avoid burnout in your ministry, this book is for you.

Maybe your burnout stems from serving under a senior pastor or ministry leader faltering in their ministry, and the struggle of walking with them despite how they are leading is wearing thin. Perhaps this book was placed in your hand by God's design so that you may learn how to counsel with or pray for them. After all, burned-out leaders are just as deserving of grace and mercy as you and me.

Books abound on toxic leadership, and all place blame on the leader for their deficiencies. Sometimes this is completely justified. But what if their toxicity stems not from moral failure or a lack of God's hand on their lives and ministry, but from the weight of the trials and difficulties of leadership? As this book helps you navigate burnout for yourself, perhaps it can also equip you to come alongside a leader facing burnout.

I ignored the symptoms and burned out. I overworked myself. I experienced all the classic burnout symptoms listed in the first paragraph. I lost sight, at times, of God's goodness and His kind intentions for me in ministry. As a church pastor and military and police chaplain, I decided it was time to take a break to regain what I had lost in my attempts to do His work my way.

Burnout is a topic many have undertaken to study and write about. I wondered what I could possibly add to the conversation that would get beyond the noise and the flurry of other books and studies on the topic. The constant encouragement of my wife and children over the years finally sank in, and I realized that I might well have unique experiences and insight that could reach ministers in ways others may not.

My story is one I am now happy to share, having realized that I indeed have something worthwhile to share. I authored a study for my doctorate that investigated the topic of burnout among police and fire chaplains, realizing as I wrote my thesis that I had been burned out for some time. So, I took the radical step of closing my church, ending my chaplaincy work, and selling my house. My wife and I bought an RV and started to travel, knowing we were not running *from* ministry, but *toward* a new expression of it.

It is my fondest wish that this book will be an encouragement to you. I hope you will rediscover God's goodness as you preach, teach, reach, counsel, and guide others in His lovingkindness. I hope you will get off the treadmill of work your ministry has perhaps become and renew yourself in His green pastures. I hope you will take my lessons and make some of them your own. I hope you will run the race fashioned for you with wisdom and renewed strength.

ENDNOTE
    1 Proverbs 9:9.

CHAPTER ONE

MY BURNOUT STORY

*"I am the door; if anyone enters through Me, he will
be saved, and will go in and out, and find pasture."* [1]

"[Spiritual Injury is] **the condition where one's spiritual
identity is in question**. *The individual suffering from
spiritual injury has difficulty understanding how his or
her view of faith, spirituality, relationship with God, and
God's involvement in one's life can be true given the
horrific experiences observed. A person suffering from
spiritual injury doesn't have answers to the questions
related to the trauma he or she has experienced, is
unsure how to resolve this tension and find the answers,
and/or may be doubting that God is trustworthy."* [2]

Have you ever said, "I feel burned out"? Maybe you don't even know
fully what burnout is, but you feel it. You have dedicated yourself
to ministry, but you find yourself feeling distant from the God you are
serving and from the people you serve. You have done so much for
the Lord, yet you do not presently feel His approval. You have made

a difference in the Kingdom, but you seem to be missing out on the satisfaction that should be the reward of your hard work. Most of all, you get that uneasy feeling that everything is unraveling before your eyes. This book is written for you.

As I was pondering what I could share that would bring hope and healing to those laboring in the fields for the Lord, God showed me the image of a wild stallion on a treadmill. You've felt His power and His calling. You have had that overwhelming urge to run fast. It was once a burden on your heart that you certainly thought would be well received and lead to glorious riches—the spiritual kind, not financial. Anyone entering ministry hoping to get rich in worldly wealth did not count the cost up front. Ministry is not designed to set you up in a high tax bracket. In a very real sense, it is about pouring out your life for others. You ran the race regardless because you knew that you could not do anything else and be satisfied. You were indeed called of God. Yet, like a horse on a treadmill (as silly as that image may be), you feel like you are sprinting hard but going nowhere.

Perhaps you experienced satisfaction initially—your ministry honeymoon period. Everyone loved your sermons, prospered from your counsel, and spoke highly of your stature in the Lord. Then it all became work. Moments of satisfaction arose from time to time as you saw people respond to your ministrations, but then those you served ran off and did something unthinkable. They engaged in extra-marital affairs. They left the church without a word of explanation or thanks. They complained and built cliques that sought to undermine you. They evaluated you harshly. They bit you, and they bit hard. As shepherds know, sheep tend to bite.

We often joke that "Ministry would be great *if* it weren't for the people!" Over time those feelings that you were making a difference came fewer and farther between. Before long, you wondered what in the world you had gotten yourself into. You questioned your calling. Maybe you even left the ministry because of the disappointment, betrayals, and what seemed to be a long slog toward heartache and a futile end. The words, "Well done, good and faithful servant," seemed too far off to carry you through the trials and loneliness of ministry.

This book is for you, friend.

You are a stallion. You are filled with an indomitable spirit that was made to run free. Somehow, someone, somewhere along the line, fenced in the land. Your pasture became smaller and the fences higher. Pretty soon, it felt like you were trapped on a treadmill. Marriages failed in spite of your prayers and counsel. Children—perhaps your own—left the church after they left home. People came, enjoyed your ministry for a time, but then moved on. You never built that megachurch. You watched as people died in your hospital, no matter how many people you recruited to the prayer chain to cry out for healing. The institutions you served heaped rules and regulations and paperwork on you that made a burden of the work you started with such great fervor. The treadmill kept moving faster, but you found your legs were quickly giving out.

Do not fear. You are in great company.

- **John the Baptist** had the most fruitful ministry in Israel in over 400 years. Thousands came to be baptized by him and heard his message of repentance. He knew his calling was to prepare the way of the Lord. The Lord Himself even showed up to be baptized! And yet John found himself alone in a jail cell for doing exactly what he was built to do.

  John ran hard. He was positioned to call out sin in the royal chambers. He was wild and free—until he wasn't. Suddenly unsure of his place in God's plan, he sent two of his disciples to ask Jesus, "Are you the Coming One, or are we to look for another?"[3]

- **Elijah** had just vanquished all the false prophets of Ahab and Jezebel when he felt he must flee for his life. Despite the powerful ministry experience of calling down fire from the Lord to consume both sacrifice and altar, after mocking the vain efforts of the many prophets arrayed against him, he despaired over a mere man's threat against his life. He shared his frustration and fear with God: "Enough! Now, Lord, take my life, for I am no better than my fathers."[4]

- **Jonah**, after one of the greatest revival ministries to the reluctant in history, also fled. He was distraught that God had used him to reach the hated Assyrians. He sat mourning the loss of shade under a withering plant, pondering how awful was his calling: "So now, LORD, please take my life from me, for death is better to me than life."[5]

> **MANY MINISTERS HAVE GONE BEFORE YOU AND HAVE FOUND THEMSELVES LOST, NO MATTER HOW GREAT THE VICTORIES THEY HAD EXPERIENCED.**

Many ministers have gone before you and have found themselves lost, no matter how great the victories they had experienced. Many have toiled in distant lands, never to be heard from again, their efforts known only to Heaven. Some, like Stephen, found their preaching utterly rejected and met their life's end at a time very close to their ministry's beginning. How much more could Stephen have done had he escaped his execution? How many more could John have baptized unto repentance? Why had Elijah's demonstration of power not led to an immediate, national revival? Why was Jonah's prophetic gift given to a people who had murdered so many of his own countrymen? And why do you and I fret so over our "light and momentary" trials when they seem insignificant compared to what others have suffered?

First of all, your suffering is not light. You have felt the sting of disappointment. You have put in the time and effort. You have done everything you were called to do. While others are basking in success in ministry, you have hoed and raked and plowed and sown, with seemingly little to show for it. Trust me: your feelings are not lost on God. Therefore, secondly, your suffering has not gone unnoticed by the One who called you. He has not forgotten you. He has never left you, never forsaken you. You are still His precious child. Nothing is lost on Him. Nothing you have offered Him is wasted.

A CLEAR SIGN

The start of my journey into burnout is hard to pin down. I am not even sure I am completely through it—not completely on the other side, whatever that looks like. However, I can locate where it became evident in a single, horrific event. I was a police chaplain, riding with one of the assistant chiefs of the police department of my city when the call came out. A vehicle accident had left an unknown number of people trapped in their truck. Arriving on the scene, we saw that it was much worse than what the radio had dispatched. First reports are always wrong. Concrete workers had been cutting on the support of an overpass. Despite the clear need to shut down the roadway beneath as they worked, they had cut away a tremendous, multiple-ton section of concrete, which came crashing down onto an SUV passing under the structure.

The scene was devastating. The concrete beam had struck directly across the cab, on top of the front and rear seats, flattening it completely to the ground. It was evident that no one could have survived. We could not get close enough to the vehicle to check on the occupants, as the workers feared that more concrete, hanging precariously by the rebar above, could collapse at any moment. It would end up taking hours to reinforce the overpass enough to permit any extraction efforts. Police, fire, medical, and construction workers all began making calls, frantic to summon help in case there was time to save lives.

I was given a sheet of paper by one of my officers. It held the vehicle owner information obtained from a quick check of the rear license plate. I stared at it for a moment, thinking how familiar the names sounded. I could not immediately place how I knew them for several minutes. In a moment, a dread realization came over me, and my heart sank. The owners were my two sons' youth pastors. Their senior pastor was a good friend. I knew his story—that he had lost a youth worship leader to a drunken driver just five years before—and I knew how this would rock his world and that of his church. I mechanically began making calls, first to a fellow chaplain for assistance, and then the dreaded call to Pastor James. However, that was only the beginning—the first twenty minutes of what would be a slowly unfolding, emotionally eviscerating, twelve-hour trauma.

As I am writing, I realize that this is the first time I have really told the story. The images, the devastated families, my boys' faces when I got home twelve hours later, and the inevitable questions of God's sovereignty, goodness, and plan swirl in my memories. Let me be clear: this was not to become a case of PTSD. It was a traumatic incident, to be sure, fraught with post-traumatic stress. However, Post-Traumatic Stress and its associated disorder are very different from burnout. This accident was to be the singular event that began to unravel years of church and trauma ministry that I had engaged since I felt and understood my call to ministry in 1995. In the twenty years between my calling and this incident, I had responded to numerous fatalities as a police chaplain in my city, served through many such horrifying scenes as a police officer, conducted combat casualty ministry for dozens of soldiers and airmen as an Army chaplain in Iraq and Afghanistan, and tended to the losses and struggles of the people of my own small church.

It wasn't long before we had tracked down the likely losses in the truck. The youth pastors weren't home. It was a Monday, and that was their day to take a trip to the local hardware store to continue their home improvement projects. Their other car was still in the garage. No one was watching their one-year-old child, so it appeared that he was with his parents. Worst of all, neither responded to text or social media messages. In a world as connected as ours had become, that was the most disheartening sign. As the hours passed and no one texted back or called to check in, the word was quickly getting out, and people were starting to ask questions it would be unwise to answer until extraction crews could get to the truck.

If you have been called on to provide this kind of support, you know how it goes. Family members started arriving. They were frantic for news and had not yet heard from their loved ones. Church members gathered, praying for the best but preparing for the worst. The local media showed up. To their credit, they remained at bay, knowing that answers would not come soon. Calls needed to be made to family and friends that had not yet heard. Ministry was happening, but it felt like that treadmill was suddenly rolling faster and faster. I was winded. My fellow chaplain, Stan, was winded. Pastor James was winded. But we had many more laps to complete before this race was finished.

Finally, more than ten hours later, the horrific news we feared was confirmed. Father, wife, and child had been killed instantly. We consoled ourselves in the knowledge that, as perfect as the timing was and as devastating the blow, they were probably completely unaware of what had happened. One moment, they were on their way to the store; in the next, they were standing with Jesus. Even the smallest of these consolations provided enough breath to keep pace on the ever-quickening treadmill. Once all the notifications had been made, the public affairs officer would make the dreadful announcement before the media.

When it was over, I went home utterly exhausted. I was met by my concerned wife and two teenage boys I had been too busy to talk to as they awaited the news. That death notification was probably the worst one I had ever delivered, as I had almost nothing left in me to provide comfort for them. In the days to come, I ministered to the officers who had been on scene, worked with Pastor James on the memorial service, attended critical incident debriefs, and walked with my kids through challenges of theodicy—questions of God's providence, power, and goodness. I also wrestled in my own mind and spirit with how God could let such an awful thing happen to such amazing young people. After all, they were just starting in ministry and impacting so many teens—all for Him. "Are you the Coming One, or am I to look for another?" "Enough! Maranatha! Come now, Lord Jesus, for this world offers nothing but death." Running started to seem a viable option, but I felt trapped. After all, people needed me, right?

As time progresses, things always transition to a "new normal." However, this did not happen so quickly for several families who had just lost their family members, pastors, or good friends. But for most of us, life returned to normal. I began to notice a subtle, steady change over the next several years. Well, I suppose I should say that I notice it clearly *now*. I probably was not as aware of the progression until much later along the timeline.

More tragedy followed. A well-loved officer on our force died in a snowmobile accident, shaking the department for months. A drowning in our local lake rattled several of our officers who had attempted to rescue the young man but failed to find him beneath the waters. I began to feel distant, unable to siphon off more of me to meet the growing need of the department. That feeling seemed to bleed into other areas of my life. I struggled to slow the treadmill, but it kept speeding up. I couldn't even see the open fields any longer. It was just me, focusing on my pounding heart while trying to keep my legs churning.

Life was changing all around me. I was suddenly traveling for work more than ever. This gave me the needed excuse to not be around people as often, even while guilt for being absent crept in. I had grown to love the people of my church, but we weren't expanding in number. My people were growing, so I felt satisfaction in that, but it pained me that we weren't effectively reaching out. I could do little more to affect change in that situation because of work. My children were aging out and leaving the house to discover their own destinies, which still carried the kind of drama that required the love and attention of their parents. Ministry became work instead of mission, activity instead of presence, duty and not desire.

MINISTRY BECAME WORK INSTEAD OF MISSION, ACTIVITY INSTEAD OF PRESENCE, DUTY AND NOT DESIRE.

A COMPLICATION

Then came the COVID-19 era. Our nation's responses to the pandemic defied logic, science, and God. Churches all around me, pastored by people I had called friends and partners in Kingdom work, were happy to go online for months. Some closed for over a year—abandoning those most in need of in-person ministry because our governor had told them by his policies that churches were non-essential. Abortion clinics, liquor stores, home improvement stores, and pot shops all were essential, but not the assembling of God's people for worship, nurture, communion, baptisms, and fellowship.

The church that was the source from which I drew my spiritual sustenance also fell in line with government mandates, abandoning two of my children who attended their school, offering online attendance only. For a school that taught such intimate healing, worship, and prayer ministry techniques, it seemed counter-intuitive that they would so readily depart from Jesus' example of touching lepers and healing the sick and instead enforce State-mandated isolation. It was as if they could not see their students' essential and imminent need for fellowship. I saw quite vividly how that hurt my children. Chaplaincy ministries of all types followed the same pattern as the churches, replacing face-to-face grief ministry with phone and video calls. The American church had lost touch with the hurting and the broken. Obedience to government had replaced obedience to God.

And then the betrayals poured in. A couple who had helped found and lead our church decided that they could not let their new business be seen as affiliated with a church defying the governor's authority by meeting in person, so they left. A group I had founded and built to bring church leaders in our area together was co-opted by another couple. The rest of the group's leadership followed, moving the ministry inward and becoming no more than a small group with no outward focus. The mandate that had been my vision ceased completely, and those I had counted as friends in the ministry simply ceased calling.

In my military chaplaincy, a disgruntled former employee had filed a baseless complaint against me, sparking a year-long legal battle that sidelined me in one of the most rewarding positions of my career—and right in the middle of the COVID-19 pandemic, when the need was greatest. The leadership of our nation's military chaplains appeared powerless and silent in the face of mounting moral and ethical challenges that impacted our fighting forces. It seemed as if most of the leadership of American Christian institutions were either "going along to get along" or fully on board with shutting down the prophetic voice and letting the government run the church.

Every sign pointed to the need to take flight. So, take flight, I did. I first ran toward a Doctor of Ministry degree. This pursuit brought a spark of life back to my soul. It taught me that not all those who are fleeing are running away. During my degree program, I began making plans to work with the Tanzanian military, focusing my doctoral thesis on the developmental processes of their chaplaincy program. Then COVID changed those plans. I had to think quickly on my feet when a professor gave our class the assignment of presenting the problem statement for our theses. By then, I had not yet even thought beyond my Tanzanian chaplaincy plan that had so recently fallen through—bringing me the long way around to why I am writing this book.

I was an instructor for the Tacoma-Pierce County Chaplaincy's Police and Fire Chaplain's Training Academy (PFCTA), where I taught a class on suicide intervention. I had taken to polling the students in each class to find out how many had not been affirmed for their call to chaplaincy by their church or denomination. Typically, about one-quarter to one-third would raise their hands. Chaplaincy is kind of the third rail of ministry in most traditions. They are not quite seen as pastors, yet they perform many pastoral duties such as marital and grief counseling, funeral and memorial services, Bible studies, and religious services. "Real" pastors don't know what to do with chaplains since they don't do their work within the four walls of the church.

To many pastors, chaplains are puzzling. They are kind of like foreign missionaries who stubbornly keep showing up at church on Sunday mornings. And, as if threatening their pastors' pulpits, some chaplains have more education and training than their pastors. Alternately, some chaplains seem to have no formal ministry training at all. At denominational meetings, pastors would joke with those who had become chaplains, asking them, "So, when did you decide to leave the ministry?"

As both a pastor and a chaplain in the police and military sectors, I have seen the two ministries as complimentary; but just try and convince both sides to sit down at the table together, and you might find a degree of uncertainty, and sometimes even animosity, between the two. In a healthy ministerial relationship, pastors and chaplains become partners, but this seemed to be the exception rather than the rule.

Oh, yes. Please forgive me. I was thinking quickly on my feet before I went down that rabbit trail. When my doctoral studies professor asked me to share my problem statement, I immediately thought of the poll I had taken of my students. I thought of the sorrow they shared with me about being pushed aside by their church leadership, as if their ministry was not *real ministry* because many in the church today are uncomfortable with their ministers hanging out amongst unsaved police officers, firefighters, medics, doctors, nurses, or military members. They don't know what to think of chaplains who quietly share their faith in the business world, with hydroplane and stock car racers, or even among those at horse racing tracks or casinos. Whatever it was that gave at least one-quarter of the chaplains in my classes cause for anguish in their home churches; my problem statement quickly developed into an investigation of the chaplain's relationship with their church leadership on chaplaincy ministry burnout.

ACCEPTING THE CHALLENGE

Once it solidified in my mind, the thesis topic became somewhat of an obsession. I read widely and deeply on burnout. It is a topic that has long gained a tremendous amount of attention in psychological circles, focusing largely on burnout in the helping professions—medical, counseling, social services, teaching, and clergy. However, there was little material at the time to work with regarding police and fire chaplaincy. In fact, mine became the first academic study on the topic. How could I have been so lucky as to break new academic ground?

Quite clearly, God had pointed me in the right direction, as I am not that clever. I began aggregating literature on burnout in general, in military and hospital chaplaincy, in law enforcement, and in firefighters. As I started planning my study, which would ultimately include 27 chaplains serving various Washington State police and fire agencies, I found the Francis Burnout Inventory (FBI). Dr. Leslie Francis is one of the most published researchers in the realm of clergy burnout. He developed the FBI, a diagnostic tool that assesses comparative levels of burnout across various ministry groups. I will discuss the FBI (please try not to get it confused with the federal agency bearing the same acronym) in more detail later in the book.

Between my reading and the conduct of my study using the FBI, some nagging questions began to encroach on my conscience. Had I become a victim of burnout? Was I honestly assessing symptoms I was experiencing when I answered the questions in the FBI for myself? Did I see myself, my feelings, and my actions in the responses of the chaplains in the study? The clear answer kept coming back, "Yes. You are burned out." Later, we'll discuss the differences between burnout, PTSD, compassion fatigue, and emotional exhaustion. They each have different components that often overlap, and it can be difficult to tell (without a good counselor) into which category your responses to your life stressors place you.

HOW CAN WE KNOW HOW TO APPLY GODLY COMFORT TO OTHERS IF WE CANNOT IDENTIFY OUR OWN AFFLICTIONS, AND HOW THEN MIGHT WE OFFER OTHERS A WAY OUT OF THEIR SORROW, GRIEF, AND PAIN?

I am not partial to "diagnosing" people with one or the other or any of the listed struggles. However, it sometimes helps to identify what you are feeling by a single word or phrase. It reassures you that others understand what you are going through. It is comforting to know that others have felt the same way. After all, the God of all comfort "comforts us in all our affliction so that we will be able to comfort those who are in any affliction with the comfort with which we ourselves are comforted by God."[6] How can we know how to apply godly comfort to others if we cannot identify our own afflictions, and how then might we offer others a way out of their sorrow, grief, and pain?

Though defining things is important, I do not advocate carrying labels around. What Heaven has not given, I must not keep. I believe we should only label afflictions as a tool to help us recognize a problem and find a path toward healing. The label, "I am burned out" is not a life sentence. PTSD must ultimately become Post Traumatic Growth. Compassion fatigue should advance toward compassion renewal. I am emphatic with my congregation about never saying "my cancer" or "my diabetes." To me, these are intruders, not possessions. I *refuse* to identify with them, as God did not give them to me. I will never tell you that you "have" burnout. I encourage you not to own any label; just realize you've merely leased it for diagnostic purposes only and must turn it back in as soon as possible.

So yes, I was burned out. I did not intend to stay burned out. It was nice to know that it had been studied and that people knew where it came from and how to get out of it. And no, I am not going to bore you with academic details of the study (although I'll include just a little for the stats nerds), as I want this book to be a healing, practical read, not something you keep by the bedside to help you get to sleep. What my chaplains shared through the course of my study is deeply insightful, particularly revelatory, and sneakily hopeful.

I want to address this book to anyone in ministry—not just chaplains and pastors. Wherever you find yourself in ministry, including counseling, leading a Bible study, or running a Christian coffee shop, I hope you will learn some practical truths about what burnout is, how it creeps up on you, how it affects your life and ministry, and how to either avoid it or heal from it. I have learned that its symptoms are unavoidable over the life of your ministry, but it doesn't mean you have to burn out completely. If you do, however, I want you to know that it need not be the death of your calling, "for the gifts and the calling of God are irrevocable."[7]

I am still running. My wife and I closed our church, sold our house, bought an RV, and are currently traveling the country trying to encourage others we meet along the way, even as we seek God's guidance as to what ministry awaits. You might call our present work a sort of "RV chaplaincy." I am no longer on the treadmill, by the way. I am finding my feet in His pasture once again. My strength is returning. "Running the race laid out for you" does not mean running on the treadmill in the same place you've always been.

Sometimes it is the fear of change, and sometimes it is a myopic focus on just what is right in front of us that keeps us in place too long. There we find ourselves treading the same ground over and over, hoping for different results—the definition of insanity. It is not bad to run away, as long as you know you are running *toward* something. My heartfelt prayer is to help you get off the treadmill and find the door again for yourself, and there you may go in and out and stretch your legs as you find pasture.

ENDNOTES

1   John 10:9.

2   Jaisen E. Fuson, "A pastoral counseling model for leading post-combat Christian soldiers experiencing spiritual injury to spiritual health through examining the biblical concepts of evil, pain, abandonment, and forgiveness" (Ph.D. diss., Biola University, Ann Arbor, 2013), abstract, Biola University, Ann Arbor.

3   Luke 7:20.

4   1 Kings 19:4.

5   Jonah 4:3.

6   2 Corinthians 1:4.

7   Romans 11:29.

CHAPTER TWO

AM I BURNED OUT?

"Come to Me, all who are weary and heavy-laden, and I will give you rest. Take My yoke upon you and learn from Me, for I am gentle and humble in heart, and you will find rest for your souls. For My yoke is easy and My burden is light." [1]

"Many clergy enter the ministry because they believe that they have been called to use their gifts to lead churches, relying upon the grace of God to cover their inadequacies. They aim for no less than leading their congregants to compassionate mission, committed evangelism, and holy living. However, many clergy experience burnout. Burnout refers to a decline in energy, motivation, and commitment and occurs when high expectations for achievements do not come to fruition despite devotion to a cause or way of life, especially in contexts of low pay and poor recognition for efforts." [2]

FOUR STORIES[3]

Story 1

Pastor Jim did all the right things. He had planted his church with the help of his denomination, attended all the right conferences to learn about church growth, completed his Master of Arts in Theology, and gathered a strong staff to help lead his fledgling work. For several years, the church steadily grew to about fifty, and it appeared to be ready to break out. Jim had found a solid associate pastor who brought a dynamic worship leader with real musical talent with him. He had great teachers leading home Bible studies and Sunday School classes. While it took a lot of work to set up for services each week in the school he was renting, it was a very good arrangement and suited the needs of a burgeoning congregation.

Then the troubles set in. Jim's busy, full-time job limited the time he could put in on weekdays. Therefore, he often stayed up late on Saturdays to craft his Sunday messages—a pastoral no-no. The arrangement wasn't ideal. A youth pastor he found came with wounds from a previous church experience that had burned him out. Still, Jim pushed him to take on more responsibility, despite signs that he and his family needed rest.

The church was well funded, but they could not find a good spot to build a permanent facility, which was a source of constant frustration. One location after another turned up empty, demoralizing Jim's people. Morale hit a new low when he found a viable but expensive property. If he also built a parsonage on the property, he could make it work financially, but that wasn't going over well with his family. At one point, they reached one hundred and fifty members, but "legacy" founders seemed to fight for control of every decision.

A favorite associate pastor announced his resignation. The worship leader became vocally critical of Jim's focus on his job over the church, and Jim fired him. The youth pastor's marriage was falling apart. His wife had an affair with one of the worship team members, crushing their family, destroying their marriage, and signaling many in the church that it was time to leave.

Jim started to distance himself from his people. He began to accuse others of undermining his authority and vision. His remaining associate pastor resigned, leaving Jim stranded with dubious support—a new, inexperienced, untrained youth pastor who upset parents with questionable methods. Sunday attendance dropped rapidly, and more families left every month. Excitement over locating a viable property for the church fizzled quickly as the other issues took their toll.

Jim left ministry altogether in frustration. The church survived another year and then folded.

Story 2

Chaplain Scott was a brand-new Army chaplain. He gained a rather elite assignment with an explosive ordnance disposal battalion and was sent to Afghanistan within a year of taking on his new position. He loved his soldiers, and they loved him, but a year of battlefield casualties, including two from his battalion, left him exhausted. Their second combat loss came just weeks before they redeployed home. His soldiers still needed him, but he had little left to give other than share in their mutual grief.

His replacement chaplain found him mostly absent from any activity except hanging out with his own battalion. Chaplain Scott offered little help orienting the new arrivals to the battlespace ministry demands, and the replacement chaplain immediately saw from Scott's mood swings, his association with his troops' trauma, and his refusal to welcome the new unit as signs that he needed ministry as badly as his men.

Chaplain Scott ultimately made it back home and got help. He recovered his capacity for ministry and moved successfully to positions where he could care for soldiers in a wartime environment.

Story 3

Chaplain Joe was a caring, compassionate hospital chaplain. He organized Bible studies, performed individual counseling, and kept up with his daily administrative duties. He had come to ministry late in life and was given a position above his experience level. He began to struggle with routine tasks and reacted by focusing only on things he deemed important, countering the instructions of his superiors. Pressures at home exacerbated the stress he faced at work. A poor evaluation and subsequent professional counseling sent him into fight or flight mode. As often happens when one is cornered, Joe did a little of both. He distanced himself from his peers and became combative with those trying to help him.

Joe recruited people in the hospital—people who cared for him and trusted his ministry—to sympathize with his growing sense of victimization. He began to isolate himself from anyone who did not immediately and fully take his side. He filed complaints against his bosses and sought opportunities to flee his situation into new assignments.

He began drinking to forget his woes, expressed a desire to suicide[4], and sought out sexual affairs to soothe his self-imposed isolation. The system ultimately helped Joe avoid accountability but did not guide him to healing for his emotional wounds. His career narrowed to mere desk work without personal ministry contact, and his troubles followed him to his future positions.

Story 4

It was my first wartime deployment. My brigade deployed to Iraq amid a rising insurgency. My battalion was assigned to Camp Victory, a heavily fortified base tucked between Baghdad and the Baghdad International Airport on what US media would declare the "most IED'ed highway in Iraq," Route Irish.[5] With time to direct my entire focus on ministry to my soldiers, I began setting up what would become a daunting schedule. On Sundays, I ran my battalion chapel service at 8 am, assistant pastored the 10 am Gospel Service on base, and finished the day leading the Pentecostal service at 6 pm. I also ran Bible studies and attended daily combat briefings, advising the commander and staff on all issues pertaining to morale, morals, ethics, and religion on the battlefield.

I started a 12-step program for soldiers with addictions made worse in a combat zone. I rode with our convoys along Route Irish into the Green Zone in Baghdad weekly to visit a platoon of our soldiers. On top of all that, I maintained counseling hours and conducted visitations to troops at their various assignments on Camp Victory. Sadly, our unit suffered mounting combat losses and injuries over time, all of which required an attentive chaplain.

Ministry was not merely abundant; it was enriching. It was addictive. But I also made time for video calls home to my wife and four young children. I was torn between two worlds. My heart longed to be home with them, especially as problems arose that I could not fix, but I was thriving doing combat ministry. I kept up this pace for eleven months. I did not realize how much stress I had been carrying until my tour ended, and I spent eight days with half of our unit with nothing to do but wait for a ride home on an airplane. When we arrived at Camp New York in Kuwait, it was as if all that stress suddenly made its appearance in my soul.

I developed physical and spiritual woes that plagued me throughout the whole eight days. I acquired what was euphemistically known as "the Kuwaiti crud," a severe head cold accompanied by an unceasing headache and other sinus cold symptoms. Quite unexpectedly, I also became viscerally angry. I did not know where the anger came from or how to overcome it. I was just mad all the time. I didn't want my soldiers to see me in that state, so I isolated myself, sleeping most of the time or wandering the camp in a rage-filled haze. I knew I was toxic, but I couldn't shake it. These afflictions began to clear a day or two before we finally got our ride home. The Kuwaiti crud left me. The anger mostly subsided but took about six months after getting home to evaporate—at least mostly.

BURNOUT, PTSD, EMOTIONAL EXHAUSTION, AND COMPASSION FATIGUE

Researchers Dr. Christine Maslach and Dr. Michael Leiter have conducted extensive studies on burnout for over 30 years. They defined burnout early on as "the index of the dislocation between what people are and what they have to do. It represents an erosion in values, dignity, spirit, and will—an erosion of the human soul." Put simply, burnout is what happens when you have high expectations of accomplishment, but the results of your efforts over time, whether real or perceived, do not match those expectations. Dr. Maslach developed a tool for assessing burnout among professionals called the Maslach Burnout Inventory. It is the gold standard today for non-clergy professionals. I will discuss in the next chapter how her diagnostic tool led to Dr. Leslie Francis' adaptation of the MBI to ministry professionals.

When you dedicate yourself to a mission, especially to the care of souls pursued based on a felt calling from God, your enthusiasm may outstrip your wisdom, resulting in burnout. Simply put, you overwork yourself. However, more often than not, burnout comes through a slow, steady erosion of your emotional energy when your desire for results falls short or your efforts are not recognized. Your emotional reserves are sapped as your ministrations appear to be failing to gain any traction. You start to see only the accumulating difficulties or failures, losing sight of your victories. Your motivation to continue begins to decline, leaving you with the feeling that it is all simply rote, meaningless activity.

WHEN YOU DEDICATE YOURSELF TO A MISSION, ESPECIALLY TO THE CARE OF SOULS ... YOUR ENTHUSIASM MAY OUTSTRIP YOUR WISDOM, RESULTING IN BURNOUT.

This negative cycle causes you to begin to detach, especially from people, but also from the work itself. Internally, you start looking for a way out. It becomes easy to devolve into a sense of lack of appreciation or accomplishment. Those feelings then get directed outward toward others as anger, resentment, frustration, shame, guilt, and avoidance. Cynicism about ministry and the people in your charge is often a good indicator that you are well on your way to complete burnout. When it reaches its peak, burnout can lead to a complete departure from ministry, an abandonment of your calling, and an unshakeable feeling of failure.

Every minister experiences at least some symptoms of burnout along their journey. The spiritual care of people is a great burden to navigate, but this can often be offset by the sense of calling that launched you into ministry. Many studies have found that clergy seem to acquire a sense of personal accomplishment that counterbalances the emotional exhaustion they experience. It is presumed that the sense that God has called them to their work creates this high level of resilience. Not every pastor, chaplain, missionary, or Bible study leader will burn out completely in the course of their work. It is when they fail to see the warning signs and correct their course that they risk experiencing the feelings of futility and frustration that lead to the abandonment of their call. In the coming chapters, I will discuss ways to diagnose your burnout symptoms and make course corrections.

Pastor Jim is a classic example of burnout. Even though a series of professional missteps and typical people problems adversely affected his pastorate, his ministry was impactful. Part of Jim's failure was not seeing where he needed help and, therefore, not being aware to ask for it. His autocratic leadership style agitated his subordinate pastors and other church leaders to frustration. The worship leader spoke out harshly against him, though he never did so publicly. One associate pastor left as he saw that he had no freedom to minister within his own giftings and felt that he had no voice in leadership. The youth pastor and his family needed professional help, but Jim thought himself able to counsel them alone, without such assistance. Attempts to encourage positive change were rebuffed. It wasn't that Pastor Jim was a bad pastor. Rather, as the pressure mounted, he began trying to control and compartmentalize the problems and problem people without trusting the help he had available to him. He had unwittingly moved from pastureland to treadmill and developed a near-sighted focus on problem-solving. When it all unraveled, he fled.

It is an all-too-common story in pastoral ministry.

Chaplain Scott suffered from compassion fatigue. He had spent his tour in Afghanistan pouring out compassion for soldiers, in some cases losing them to injury or death. While those incidents also brought about post-traumatic stress, they did not ultimately lead him to the clinical disorder (PTSD) that often comes with such trauma. He did not experience any of the trauma of his soldiers directly. However, in his counseling and care for them, he did experience what compassion fatigue is often referred to as—secondary traumatic stress (STS). He did not witness his soldiers killed, but he did engage in intense, emotional periods where he guided fellow soldiers through grief with counseling, memorial services, ramp ceremonies[6], and ongoing forms of group critical incident stress debriefings.

Chaplain Scott was reaching the end of his tour. While he had courageously carried his Gospel calling out for his unit for a whole year, the sense of his mission's conclusion allowed him to feel the full weight of compassion fatigue. He had nothing left to give his soldiers, much less a new unit that had not experienced what they had been through together.

His irritability with the incoming chaplain was completely understandable. His detachment from the mission, including helping the new chaplain acclimate to the combat environment, was to be expected. Home is often the best remedy for compassion fatigue for military chaplains redeploying from the combat zone. While they, like their soldiers, may be at risk of PTSD, they often recover and reset in time for the next deployment. The onset of compassion fatigue is often sudden, as it was for Chaplain Scott. You know it the moment it hits you. Burnout, on the other hand, develops slowly over time and is often missed until it has fully settled in.

THE ONSET OF COMPASSION FATIGUE IS OFTEN SUDDEN. YOU KNOW IT THE MOMENT IT HITS YOU. BURNOUT, ON THE OTHER HAND, DEVELOPS SLOWLY OVER TIME AND IS OFTEN MISSED UNTIL IT HAS FULLY SETTLED IN.

Chaplain Joe is an example of PTSD, though not from his job conditions. Traumatic experiences earlier in his life had settled into the disorder. Everything that followed became a trigger that reopened the old wounds and pushed him into a defensive posture. Every new insult to his capabilities brought back the traumas of yesteryear, arousing his fight or flight response. Fear was his driving motivation, causing him to harden his outer shell as protection from perceived attacks. He openly spoke of nightmares, sleeplessness, depression, anxiety, and suicidal thoughts, yet he refused to make himself available to those around him who might help him. He still mustered the compassion to perform ministry tasks and was faithful to his Bible studies and chapel duties. He was not suffering from compassion fatigue or burnout but from the invasion of old traumas that changed his lens, keeping him from seeing his present, workable circumstances with perspective. Post-traumatic stress is often referred to as a normal response to an abnormal (or traumatic) event. When not properly treated, or when the traumas compound, it can lead to a serious psychological disorder (PTSD). I will not be discussing PTSD in detail in this book.

MY STORY

At the end of my Iraq tour, my symptoms were very similar to Chaplain Scott's. We each likely suffered from both compassion fatigue and emotional exhaustion. The two are very difficult to distinguish, except in retrospect. At the end of my eleven months in Iraq, which had followed four months of training away from my family, I was emotionally drained. I had no energy left to engage with my soldiers, much less to minister to them for those eight days.

I felt trapped and unable to get out of my funk. One day, as I was wandering around the camp where we were interned, I saw that the chapel was showing the movie *Luther*, a film about the life of Martin

Luther. I slipped quietly into the back of the dark chapel to watch and try to get my mind off my situation. I remember God speaking to a deep place in me as I saw Martin's trials played out in the film, and under the cover of darkness, I wept. My physical symptoms matched my emotional state. My body was spent, and it had happened quite suddenly. Fortunately, the ensuing recovery time at home, away from my unit, was enough to replenish my emotional stores and ease my return to normal life and ministry in the civilian world.

I was not yet at burnout. However, I had already embarked on the long road to the destination. The journey was marked with small recoveries followed by new insults to my perceptions of God's goodness, provision, and calling. It would take another ten years to get to the bridge collapse, where burnout became evident. During that time, I faced a deployment to the ravaged city of New Orleans after the destruction of hurricanes Katrina and Rita, another tour of duty to Afghanistan, participation in Washington State's devastating Oso landslide response, and many more local and personal traumas, trials, and tribulations.

BURNOUT

Burnout happens over time. Dr. Maslach identified three components of burnout:

- emotional exhaustion,
- depersonalization,
- and sense of personal accomplishment.

Emotional exhaustion is the depletion of your emotional stores over time due to the constant drain of compassion ministries. One can reach compassion fatigue over a short period and yet not experience emotional exhaustion. However, repeated cycles of compassion fatigue from traumatic event responses, or even just the wear and tear of the compassion expended in your ministry over time, can lead to emotional exhaustion.

Emotional exhaustion becomes evident when you can no longer bounce back from isolated events of compassion fatigue. You lose the capacity to connect with people emotionally, sympathize or empathize, or find satisfaction in your ministry's successes. When you comfort or counsel from a place of emotional exhaustion, your advice becomes mechanical and your consolation empty. If your ministrations are effective, it is more likely that God is using you *in spite of you*, not through or because of you.

WHEN YOU COMFORT OR COUNSEL FROM A PLACE OF EMOTIONAL EXHAUSTION, YOUR ADVICE BECOMES MECHANICAL AND YOUR CONSOLATION EMPTY.

The onset of emotional exhaustion can lead to depersonalization. Depersonalization is the process of distancing oneself from others because pouring out more emotion from an empty cup is impossible. As burnout creeps in, the exhaustion you feel saps your energy to engage people in normal, everyday conversations. It becomes even more difficult when they require something of you, such as counseling, meetings, or sermons. It is all too common to become quite cynical about the people in your church, your police officers and firefighters, your hospital patients, or even your mentors and leaders. The thought of going to work in the ministry environment becomes mentally painful, and the need to escape human contact finds fruition when you call in sick just to avoid people.

Depersonalization is not limited to workers in the helping professions. Everyone can experience it. It is well evidenced in social media, where people easily forget that there is a human being on the other side of any discussion. We see it in politics, where politicians begin hurling personal insults at one another instead of debating issues. Among clergy, however, compassion, empathy, mourning with those who mourn, and the ability to pray for those in need are pastoral commodities that must be present to remain effective.

James and John learned Jesus' heart on this matter when He rebuked them for wanting to call down fire on a city of the Samaritans because they would not receive Jesus on His journey to Jerusalem. They had learned to depersonalize Samaritans from their youth. Jesus had to correct this condition in the hearts of James and John if they were to grow as disciples and fulfill the Great Commission.

When we are emotionally exhausted and start to depersonalize, it becomes much easier to dismiss the needs and humanity of others. We hear cries for help as grumbling and dissension. Fellow ministers are no longer confidants but competitors. We see divine appointments right in front of us, but we cannot push ourselves to engage them. A mix of anger, frustration, fear, sadness, and abandonment swirl beneath a pressure plate in our souls. The last thing we want is to have God expose those frayed emotions with a ministry moment that leads to a stirring miracle.

When we avoid ministry, we dismiss *people* who are on God's heart as if they were just inconvenient *tasks* to be accepted or dismissed. At times we don't even want the task. Jonah depersonalized the Assyrians. When God called him to proclaim destruction over Nineveh, Jonah knew they would repent and that God would relent. God used him *in spite of* his prophetic gift and calling. The last place we want to be in ministry is in that place where God occasionally uses us *in absentia*. God will be present for the need, even if you won't. Liberation and rescue will arise from another place[7]—and that is not the end for which you and I entered the ministry.

You've probably heard the adage, "God doesn't call the equipped. He equips the called." This is particularly evident in chaplaincy ministries, especially among first responders—police officers, firefighters, and EMTs, among other groups often the first on hazardous, dangerous, or traumatic scenes. Our spirits, minds, and bodies were not made for repeated, unrelenting, sometimes brutal traumatic incidents. Police and firefighters are well known for their vulnerability to burnout. Imagine being the chaplain who shows up to the same scenes where they show up but must also deal with grieving families who have lost a young adult child to suicide or a husband and father to a tragic auto collision.

As a cop, I had responded to it all during my career; or so it felt to me that I had. I had been to the scene of workers who had fallen over 400 feet from a crane while working on the ceiling of the Kingdome in Seattle. I had been to a dozen suicide scenes. My first one was a rather grizzly shotgun suicide. I had been to fatalities from vehicular collisions to shootings, stabbings, and horrible accidents. I rarely had to deal with the secondary victims—the families and friends of those killed, because that was the chaplain's job. Then I became a police chaplain. I can tell you that the "equipping" isn't just an innate, internal strength with which one is born. It is something God gives incident by incident to those He has called. It requires a constant dependence upon Him.

By the time police officers complete a twenty- or thirty-year career, they are often cynical to a fault. They learned early on that "everyone always lies." If you don't realize that during your rookie year, you will fail to be an effective officer. You know never to trust the first version of any story you are told. This lesson starts an officer down a path of cynicism that leads to some dark places. It is axiomatic—you don't just take someone's word for it when they tell you their side of the story. It is this inherent cynicism that makes police chaplaincy one of the hardest ministry fields of all. No one walks in as a new chaplain and expects to be accepted because they wear a uniform. They must earn it. That same cynicism can easily attach to chaplains who have responded to scene after scene, death after death.

It doesn't make it any easier that chaplains in all fields receive regular rejection of their primary ministry: the Gospel message. It is easy for chaplains to feel the weight of the constant brush-offs. Some chaplains give up and become satisfied with merely being the guy or girl that only shows up when called. They become exhausted from the trauma ministry and take the constant rejections of their faith personally. They distance themselves from officers and firefighters who need the incarnate *ministry of presence*—perhaps the only Jesus they will encounter throughout their careers. When they shrink from the fullness of their calling because some will not talk about matters of faith, chaplains miss the long-term effects their consistency, persistence, and enduring compassion have across time. Chaplaincy seldom comes with the thrills of moving altar calls and spontaneous revival meetings.

Pastors preach to the faithful. While they must still earn their congregation's trust, usually, they are joyfully welcomed when they take a new pulpit. They occasionally engage in trauma ministry or grief counseling, but the bread and butter of their work is in encouragement, teaching, and shepherding a grateful (if sometimes biting) flock. Pastoring comes with its periods of rejection, dejection, and disappointment, but it is largely removed from the traumatic events and large-scale rejection of faith common in chaplaincy. Among clergy of all types, however, an abiding sense that their work makes a difference—known in the study of burnout as *personal accomplishment*—creates a buffer between emotional exhaustion and burnout. Studies repeatedly show that, in contrast to other helping professions, clergy tend to maintain a high sense of personal accomplishment in the face of other burnout indicators. In all helping professions, maintaining this sense of positive achievement is what makes the emotional expenses worthwhile. Knowing that your work is important and helps people offsets exhaustion and builds resilience to continue helping people.

When that sense of personal accomplishment diminishes as emotional exhaustion sets in, burnout becomes almost inevitable. Pastor Jim easily overcame the trials and dramas of church ministry for several years. When both leadership and congregants started leaving, his ability to feel a sense of worth and mission dissolved. Abandonment, isolation, demoralization, and loss of ministry vision took their toll, leaving him in fight or flight mode. When the fight instinct began to fail, flight took its place. His emotional survival required it. His personal effectiveness in ministry waned, and he naturally sought a way out. Few can weather being drained spiritually and emotionally without seeing that their ministry efforts impact people.

REFLECTION

BURNOUT INDICATES THAT YOU HAVE ENGAGED IN THE FIGHT LONG ENOUGH AND WITH A HIGH ENOUGH INTENSITY TO HAVE GROWN WEARY WITH DOING GOOD.

Burnout is nothing to be ashamed of. It is not an indicator of success or failure. In fact, it indicates that you have engaged in the fight long enough and with a high enough intensity to have grown weary with doing good. God sees you—not for what you do but for who you are. His compassion toward you is great, and His mercy unfathomable. His love for you is so immense that in all of your imaginings, you have not yet fully comprehended it.

Know that God desires you to be refreshed and restored. Made whole. Made new. He called you for a reason. His faith in what He has placed in you is greater than your faith in what you carry. Extend grace to yourself right now and receive the comfort of God's peace enveloping you in this hour. Your trajectory is not entropy—moving from stasis to destruction. Your trajectory is from faith to faith, glory to glory.

"And it is my prayer that your love may abound more
and more, with knowledge and all discernment,
so that you may approve what is excellent, and so
be pure and blameless for the day of Christ, filled
with the fruit of righteousness that comes through
Jesus Christ, to the glory and praise of God."
PHILIPPIANS 1:9-11, ESV

- Consider what it means "that your love may abound still more and more." Does that describe where you are in ministry today?

- Did you see yourself in any of the stories? Are you fatigued, exhausted, cynical, or angry?

- Can you say that you are aware of who you are and what you are doing at every moment in your ministry, displaying real knowledge and discernment?

- Is your sincerity and blamelessness evident, your breastplate of righteousness intact?

PRAYER OF ENCOURAGEMENT

God, I pray that the eyes of this reader's heart may be enlightened as they progress through this book. Bring them new awareness. May they understand they are not alone and take comfort in remembering that You are the source of their supply. May their ministry bring You glory and praise as You renew them and restore the hope of their calling in Christ Jesus. Amen.

ENDNOTES

1   Matthew 11:28-30.

2   Laura Barnard and John F. Curry, "The Relationship of Clergy Burnout to Self-Compassion and Other Personality Dimensions," *Pastoral Psychology* 61 (2012): 149.

3   I have changed the names of those in these stories apart from my own. I have used only male names where a female may have been the subject. I have included no confidential information in sharing these stories.

4   Author's Note: I purposefully avoid calling suicide something we "commit," as that implies a criminal act. Most states now have decriminalized suicide and many suicidologists have ceased using "commit," seeing it as an antiquated term that creates a stigma around talking about it.

5   An IED is an improvised explosive device; explosives hidden along foot or vehicle traffic routes intended to kill or injure soldiers during their combat missions.

6   A ramp ceremony is one in which the remains of soldiers killed in combat are escorted onto an airplane for transport home to the U.S. for burial. The finality of these ceremonies, where the flag-draped casket of a comrade-in-arms flies off and the comrade is notably and permanently absent from the ranks, is palpable. While these ceremonies help provide closure, the hole left in the formation is felt for the remainder of the tour, and many feel that void for a lifetime.

7   See Esther 4:14.

CHAPTER THREE

HOW DO I KNOW IF I AM BURNED OUT?

"Test yourselves to see if you are in the faith; examine yourselves! Or do you not recognize this about yourselves, that Jesus Christ is in you—unless indeed you fail the test?"[1]

"Francis et al. (2005) argued that positive affect and negative affect are not opposite ends of a single continuum but two separate continua. Such a model explains why it is entirely reasonable for individual clergy to experience at the same time high levels of positive affect and high levels of negative affect."[2]

THE PRESSURES OF MODERN MINISTRY

One of the biggest lessons I learned from my experience, and one that was backed up by my study, is that ministers experiencing burnout often did not see it coming. Once you are in the middle of burnout, you are sprinting so fast on the treadmill, just trying to keep up with the pace of the needs around you, that you are the least likely person to notice you're about to hit a wall. The urgency of pastoral and chaplaincy work can blind you to your own need for ministry. A repeated refrain from managers of chaplains was, "Who is taking care of the chaplain?"

In the church environment, pastors are usually surrounded by other pastors on their staff, church board members, elders, deacons, prayer teams, or nearby church pastors and denominational leaders who can check in on them to ask how they are doing. Chaplains are often on their own unless they gather healthy human support structures around themselves. However, for both pastors and chaplains, their accountability partners sometimes fail to catch when they are overextended and approaching emotional exhaustion. The burden cannot always fall on friends, family, and colleagues who have their own busy lives to attend to.

The bottom line is that clergy bear the primary responsibility to develop healthy personal habits and surround themselves with people who will hold them accountable for their abilities. We often call this *self-care*. The presumption in self-care is that you cannot assume that others will rescue you from yourself. You must take responsibility for your own care if you are to run the race to the finish line.

The pressures of modern ministry work against proper self-care habits. Weekly sermon development, needy parishioners, the ever-ringing phone, home and hospital visitations, budgets, reports, mentorship of younger ministers, developing and attending programs, board meetings, and many other activity-driven responsibilities fashion us into *human doings*. Self-care is about your *being*. Church leadership has taken on a business leadership model that is not evident in scripture, and that model bleeds over into chaplaincy, elevating performance above presence.

Then there is the incredible pressure to be bigger than your ministry. Social media has changed what it means to be a pastor, a chaplain, or a Bible teacher. Teachers and professors of theology now must be information technology experts so they can navigate online student coursework. Parishioners and followers expect pastors, chaplains, missionaries, authors, and teachers to be on Facebook, Twitter, Instagram, Snapchat, and other social media outlets. As if that wasn't enough, your people expect an online service option for when they don't feel like attending church in person.

Further, if you're going to be a superstar, you must also have a podcast and a YouTube or Rumble channel. The technology required just to run an average-sized church service today is a massive effort requiring expertise that has spontaneously fashioned into its own form of ministry. Ministers of thirty years ago struggled with the amount of work they faced. They felt they had too little time to do it all. So, what are today's ministers missing out on now that technology has soaked up the time not required of yesteryear's pastors?

When the pressure to perform rises, the first thing to suffer is usually our private time with God, and that is where we get our *identity*—our sense of *being*. I've heard it said that performance ministry without God is like prostitution: you perform unnaturally those things that come naturally only through intimacy.

I'm not sure Jesus would have ventured into a podcast or video ministry had He come to our world today. He spent abundant time in solitude, leaving His disciples behind as He sought out a quiet wilderness place to commune with His Father.

> **WHEN THE PRESSURE TO PERFORM RISES, THE FIRST THING TO SUFFER IS USUALLY OUR PRIVATE TIME WITH GOD, AND THAT IS WHERE WE GET OUR *IDENTITY*—OUR SENSE OF *BEING*.**

He engaged large crowds, healed thousands, debated the Pharisees and Sadducees, and spent hours traveling on foot from one ministry venue to another. The demands on His time never interfered with His time spent in prayer. I am convinced that my burnout experience was largely driven by the most common distractors from focused prayer that all ministers face today. It took two decades of ministry for me to finally sit down and take a short test just to see what was happening to me. I was too busy to learn that I was too busy.

THE FBI

That test, the Francis Burnout Inventory (FBI), became a blessing to many of the chaplains in my study. The questions it posed forced each of them to take an honest look at how they conduct their ministries—and, more importantly, whether or not they are at risk of becoming ineffective because they are not taking proper care of themselves. Dr. Leslie Francis developed his inventory tool after he recognized that the Maslach Burnout Inventory (MBI) was not tailored precisely enough for the unique helping environment of clergy.[3] Further, his research uncovered what he called a *balanced affect* between ministry satisfaction (a sense of personal accomplishment) and emotional exhaustion.

Dr. Francis sought "to reconceptualize the notion of burnout and to propose a measure more carefully crafted to fit the experience of clergy." The MBI's three-component theory did not adequately capture the lived experience of burnout, particularly among priests and pastors, who seem to find joy in their work despite their professional experience of exhaustion. The balanced affect theory helped explain this dichotomy and the FBI helped highlight it. However, it remains true that even the most diligent minister may still ultimately succumb to the effects of burnout, no matter "the joy set before them."

The FBI consists of twenty-two questions, eleven of which comprise the SEEM component, or the Scale of Emotional Exhaustion in Ministry. The other eleven comprise the SIMS component or the Satisfaction in Ministry Scale. The latter gauges the minister's sense of personal accomplishment, while the former assesses their level of emotional exhaustion and depersonalization. Dr. Francis has repeatedly studied clergy populations and found that the intense sense of mission and effectiveness ministers experience in their work is not always diminished by high workloads, low pay, and the sometimes-low recognition they receive. Emotional exhaustion does not necessarily result in a decrease in personal accomplishment among ministers, at least not at the same rate it does among other helping professions.

In my study, however, I found a mild decrease in the sense of personal accomplishment among first responder chaplains that was impacted by emotional exhaustion. I must offer several caveats to my findings so that you don't get the idea that my study somehow contradicted Dr. Francis' *balanced affect* theory. First, my study was quite small. I had only twenty-seven participants, while Dr. Francis' studies include hundreds. The larger the study, the greater the likelihood of accurate population samples and results.

Second, there is a *ceiling effect* in measurements of personal accomplishment. So many of the respondents in my study indicated such high levels of personal accomplishment initially that, when tested a second time for burnout, there was little room left for positive change in their responses. This means that their exhaustion (SEEM) scores could vary rather broadly between the first and second tests, but their satisfaction (SIMS) scores could not. While this is good news, it makes it difficult in a smaller study to test the balanced affect theory.

Finally, my study's focus was on finding ways to improve chaplains' burnout symptoms, most notably by linking them more intimately with their home churches or denominations (what I titled their *sending sources*). While one goal was to assess improvements in burnout symptoms as relationships were built, the study's primary purpose was not to test the balanced affect. I will talk more about my study later, but for now, it might help you to know how it was structured.

The twenty-seven chaplains were not the only participants in my study. I included eleven of the chaplains' sending sources (church pastors, denominational leaders, or ecclesiastical endorsers). I sought to include all nineteen possible sending source representatives but received only eleven responses indicating a willingness to participate. Eight chaplains indicated that they were not "sent" by any particular church or sending agent. This closely approximated the number of hands that would go up when I polled students in my classes; about one quarter to two-thirds had not been affirmed in their ministry by their—or any—church or denomination.

One of the hypotheses of my study was that connection with a sending source was important in helping chaplains mitigate the effects of burnout. This may seem self-explanatory, but humans have a way of striking out and doing things on their own, detached from supportive communities who might help them. People often start businesses without connecting with a community of business builders, such as a chamber of commerce or small business agency. They thus have no one to guide and help them avoid the pitfalls that many entrepreneurs experience. It is dangerous and not entirely biblical to strike out in ministry on your own, detached from the Church. But some believe that the call to minister is so powerful that it overrides the slow processes of organized religion and the dismissals of church leadership.

However, like a business that burns hot for a moment and then crashes, so too might many find themselves faring poorly in ministry without drawing from the well of wisdom, experience, and caution that others have built over time. One must be quite careful that their stated sense of mission is not merely a covering for their wish to avoid accountability or growth through a pre-determined process. My study showed a distinct connection between a chaplain's longevity and success in ministry, the affirmation they received for their ministry at the outset, and the ongoing support they get from their church.

MY STUDY SHOWED A DISTINCT CONNECTION BETWEEN A CHAPLAIN'S LONGEVITY AND SUCCESS IN MINISTRY, THE AFFIRMATION THEY RECEIVED FOR THEIR MINISTRY AT THE OUTSET, AND THE ONGOING SUPPORT THEY GET FROM THEIR CHURCH.

Additional participants included the Board of Directors of the Tacoma-Pierce County Chaplaincy (TPCC), a chaplaincy organizational agency (COA) that helps train and vet chaplains for ministry among the agencies they serve. Like dozens of similar COAs springing up around the nation, they do not ordain or endorse chaplains, and they are not a denomination. Rather, they are a Christian agency that helps police and fire departments find chaplains and vice-versa. They also provide an excellent source of fellowship for chaplains of first responders, as this chaplain community has unique ministry experiences with which only other chaplains might empathize.

First responder ministry is unique compared to traditional chaplaincies in schools, hospitals, or the military. Thus, unlike a traditional pulpit ministry, police and fire chaplains need peers with whom they can discuss the traumas they encounter in the course of their work. Many of their experiences are hard for pastors to grasp—and even harder for the average civilian. The sheer volume of grief and trauma they work with regularly makes them more vulnerable to burnout, secondary traumatic stress, and even PTSD than ministers in conventional settings.

The exceptions to this rule may include military chaplains who perform combat ministry and hospital chaplains who work in their hospitals' Emergency Departments. The trauma ministry factor may well have been another limitation in my study's ability to assess Dr. Francis' balanced affect theory. High incident trauma response is unique to these sectors of chaplaincy. The nature of the first responder chaplain's ministry aligns them more closely with the subjects of their ministry (police and firefighters) than with their peers in other ministry sectors. Police and firefighters do not enjoy balanced affect when it comes to burnout, and it does not seem that their chaplains do, either. Instead of being tempered by a heightened sense of accomplishment, exhaustion tends to bleed their satisfaction.

The study ran for approximately four months. I started by having the chaplains complete demographic questionnaires and the FBI, including an initial question about their present perception of their level of burnout. Since they would be taking the FBI a second time a few months later, the same question was used both times. The goal was to track the chaplains' change in perception of their burnout as they learned more about burnout and engaged more intimately with their sending sources.

I also conducted focus groups with TPCC and a small group of participating chaplains who wanted to help find solutions to the burnout issue. Between iterations of the FBI, I conducted direct interviews with each chaplain alone, followed by interviews with the chaplains and their sending sources, in which only the eleven source agents participated. Of those eleven sending source representatives, only eight completed the final survey.

In my estimation, the most impactful piece of the study included the responses to the interview questions spurred by the chaplains' participation in the FBI. Before I offer some of their answers, perhaps you might like to take the FBI (following) for yourself.[4] This assessment of your current level of burnout may open your eyes to many stress responses you were unaware you were experiencing.

A few things to note:

- You will only benefit by answering each question honestly as it relates to your present ministry or ministries.

- Bear in mind that chaplains are often pastors or full-time employees in the civilian sector, in addition to their chaplaincy ministry. Pastors may have full-time or part-time jobs outside the church or be employed full-time by their church.

- Your initial scores will not give you a "yes" or "no" option of whether you are burned out or not. They simply gauge the intensity of your perception of burnout.

- It will help to compare your responses to those I will share later from the chaplains in my study.

- And, if you're like me, you'll probably jump to the point in the book where those are listed before reading on (just as you may well have skipped the earlier chapters to get here). That is perfectly acceptable. Your self-care is your responsibility. Just make sure you read the rest of the material so that you have greater context for awareness of what your results mean for you.

The following questions are about how you feel working in your present ministry. Please read the sentence carefully and think, "How true is this of me?"

AS—Agree Strongly, **A**—Agree, **NC**—Not Certain, **D**—Disagree, **DS**—Disagree Strongly

I feel drained in fulfilling my ministry roles	AS A NC D DS
I have accomplished many worthwhile things in my current ministry	AS A NC D DS
Fatigue and irritation are part of my daily experience	AS A NC D DS
I gain a lot of personal satisfaction from working with people in my current ministry	AS A NC D DS
I am invaded by sadness I can't explain	AS A NC D DS
I deal very effectively with the problems of people in my current ministry	AS A NC D DS
I am feeling negative or cynical about the people with whom I work	AS A NC D DS
I can easily understand how those among whom I minister feel about things	AS A NC D DS
I always have enthusiasm for my work	AS A NC D DS
I feel very positive about my current ministry	AS A NC D DS
My humor has a cynical or biting tone	AS A NC D DS
I feel that my ministry (chaplain/pastoral) has a positive influence on people's lives	AS A NC D DS
I find myself spending less and less time with those among whom I minister	AS A NC D DS
I feel that my ministry (chaplain/pastoral) has a positive influence on people's faith	AS A NC D DS
I have been discouraged by the lack of personal support for me here	AS A NC D DS

I feel my ministry is really appreciated by people	AS A NC D DS
I find myself frustrated in my attempts to accomplish tasks important to me	AS A NC D DS
I am really glad I entered the ministry	AS A NC D DS
I am less patient with those among whom I minister than I used to be	AS A NC D DS
The ministry here gives real purpose and meaning to my life	AS A NC D DS
I am becoming less flexible in my dealings with those among whom I minister	AS A NC D DS
I gain a lot of personal satisfaction from fulfilling my ministry roles	AS A NC D DS

There is no scoring rubric for this test to tell you where you fit on a scale of burnout. Your answers to each question are largely subjective and rely upon many variables unique to your life and ministry. If you have both a pastoral and chaplaincy ministry, it can be helpful to take the test twice, answering each question as honestly as you can specifically about each ministry. For instance, you may agree strongly that you are "really glad you entered the ministry" regarding your chaplaincy, but feel less certain about your pulpit ministry. One pastor who had a low level of burnout stated that he found his chaplaincy ministry was a nice distraction from his church responsibilities. No one in his police department complained about his sermons, the color of the carpet, or how loud the worship music was.

Perhaps you run a chaplaincy organizational agency and also function as a chaplain within that agency. A few chaplains in the study fell into this category and found that, while they were frustrated in their attempts to accomplish tasks important to them, they were not at all likewise frustrated with accomplishing tasks in their chaplaincy ministries. It can be difficult to distinguish between the stressors from our jobs and those from our ministries. However, that is what burnout is all about—it is a combination of various pressures working against your emotional resources and competing with your sense of accomplishment.

I aggregated the answers to the FBI into a quantitative analysis that you can find in the appendix (beginning on page 205) if social science studies are your cup of tea. These are good for developing statistical overviews of the responses of the study population; however, statistics seldom tell the whole story. Although we all tend to succumb to many of the same pitfalls within and experience the same joys derived from our ministries, none of us are mechanically defined by statistical analysis. So I also conducted many interviews to add a qualitative review of the participating chaplains' thoughts on burnout. These helped the study speak to the unique life and ministry circumstances in which each chaplain works.

IT IS GOOD TO KNOW THAT OTHERS FACE THE SAME CHALLENGES (AND SUCCESSES) AND EXPERIENCE THE SAME PERSONAL AND PROFESSIONAL PROBLEMS (AND JOYS) THAT WE ENCOUNTER.

It is good to know that others face the same challenges (and successes) and experience the same personal and professional problems (and joys) that we encounter. It is good to know that what is often good for the goose is also good for the gander. In the same way that all people experience catching a cold, all people also benefit from a good dose of vitamin C. As you review your responses, know that many others have been in your shoes. True, some have left the ministry in disappointment, but many have overcome the trials and run the race with endurance.

HOW THE CHAPLAINS RESPONDED TO THE FBI

Almost every chaplain in the study responded with enthusiasm to the FBI. Some indicated that it was the first time they had thought about burnout and been given a chance to assess where they might fall on the burnout spectrum. One chaplain stated:

Some of the questions speak to feeling burned out. Overall, I definitely don't feel burnt out. It's been just over four years, so I haven't been doing this very long, but this takes a lot out of you. I don't even really pretend to know the benchmark for what it takes for people to start feeling that level of burnout. I certainly don't feel it yet, but that doesn't mean there aren't days or weeks or times when I feel like there isn't a lot on my shoulders.

One participant who was surprised that he scored higher on burnout indicators stated, "It's interesting to hear that I met criteria for burnout because I maintain good self-awareness and don't meet criteria for depression or anxiety." The fact that he referenced not meeting the criteria for depression and anxiety indicated that he was trying to take stock of his emotional state; however, depression and anxiety are not necessarily symptoms of burnout. Even those who believe they are self-aware often lack the ability to see objectively from outside of their own situation. Another chaplain who had previously experienced burnout saw the FBI as a good opportunity for present reflection:

51

I felt pretty good about myself at this point. I was reading most of the questions as reminders of what to look for because, at one time, when I was burned out, I was the last one to recognize what was happening. Once you really get into it, you know, you're in denial. So this allowed me to ask the question, "Am I in denial, or can some of these things be happening?" I think it would be a good thing for most of us chaplains to take (something like the FBI) every once in a while.

Another first responder chaplain (FRC) said that the FBI helped her realize that she was burned out from her chaplaincy ministry. She stated that she had been afraid that her phone would ring for over six months. "I'm burned out from looking at dead bodies of people who've shot themselves. I'm not burned out because my pastor didn't help me enough." Another FRC recognized that he had essentially accepted burnout as part of his ministry: "I've had very little respect for a Sabbath and very low margins left over for me to have extra time. So, if I take a chaplain call, something else is getting pushed out. Because of that, I think I've been functioning at a low level of burnout essentially for a decade or so."

The difficulty of balancing ministry and life was a repeated theme, as another FRC expressed:

I'm not paying as much attention to my own well-being as I thought I was. There's a lot of talk about self-care because we talk to families and First Responders who are experiencing trauma. That's one of the first tools we have in our toolkit is to talk about self-care, so that should be one of the first tools we pull out. I had lots of talks with an instructor at the

Chaplain's Academy (PFCTA) that set me up to be conscious of my own self-care. Then I think I've maybe let it slide. I think (the Francis Burnout Inventory) exposed that I'm not valuing it like I should.

You should remember that the FBI is just a tool. Like any tool, it is only as effective as the person using it allows it to be. Honest self-reflection is essential to the FBI. No one is forcing you to read this book, and no one will check your test scores. The only "grades" that follow are how much you become aware of your present state of ministry capacity and how much healing you may seek should you find yourself struggling with burnout.

Paul challenges us: "Test yourselves *to see* if you are in the faith; examine yourselves! Or do you not recognize *this about* yourselves, that Jesus Christ is in you—unless indeed you fail the test?"[5] I am convinced that this is as applicable to seeing *where* you are in your faith as it is *whether* you are in the faith. It is a question of identity. You are either abiding in the vine, or you are not. You may find yourself slipping on the vine or perhaps unable even to remember that sense of abiding in Him that you once felt. You are not alone.

> **YOU ARE EITHER ABIDING IN THE VINE OR YOU ARE NOT—IT IS A QUESTION OF IDENTITY.**

Paul also reminds us: "No temptation has overtaken you but such as is common to man; and God is faithful, who will not allow you to be tempted beyond what you are able, but with the temptation will provide the way of escape also, so that you will be able to endure it."[6] The temptation to fall into despair is common to ministers, as Jonah, Elijah, and even John the Baptist displayed. It is incumbent upon God's shepherds to find the way of escape, if not only for their own sanity, then certainly for that of their sheep.

God's ministers share themselves in ways that other helping professionals do not. They live in fishbowls. They make themselves spiritually and emotionally vulnerable to large groups of people, and some people within those groups do not always have the minister's best interests in mind. The minister leaves their identity open to attack, betrayal, disappointment, and all manner of emotional wounds. But God's promises are good. He will not leave you without an escape plan, and He will not permit you to be tried beyond your ability to endure. Sometimes, the way is to stand firm in the ministry to which you have been called. Sometimes, as I am experiencing, the way is to run—not *away from* but rather *toward* something. If you're running away, beware of large fish.

In every possible outcome, we must always continue abiding in the Vine.

REFLECTION

You are not alone. Everyone who embraces a ministry calling ultimately experiences emotional depletion and relational isolation. We all feel unappreciated and overwhelmed at times. This feeling does not mean there is something wrong with you. In the Garden of Gethsemane, even Jesus felt abandoned. Your self-care is your responsibility, and a proper support system is essential for rounding out a good self-care plan. As you reflect upon this chapter, use it to heighten your awareness of your emotional health, both where it is right now and where you desire it to be. Remember that experiencing the symptoms of burnout is inevitable, but burning out entirely is not.

"So then, my beloved, just as you have always obeyed,
not as in my presence only, but now much more in
my absence, work out your salvation with fear and
trembling; for it is God who is at work in you, both
*to desire and to work for **His** good pleasure."*
PHILIPPIANS 2:12-13

Take the FBI if you have not already done so.

- Consider the honesty of your answers.

- Weigh your scores against the admonishment to "work out your salvation with fear and trembling," tempered by the understanding that "it is God who is at work in you."

- Are you in reverent awe of how God is working in you for **His** good pleasure?

- Do you fully appreciate the pleasure He takes in your work? In you, as His child? Or are you still trying to win His pleasure by your performance?

PRAYER OF ENCOURAGEMENT

Gracious God, I pray You will help this reader understand how they got to where they are today. Remind them that You are their loving Father and that You delight in Your children—of whom they are not at all the least. Remove all condemnation from their hearts and show them Your goodness here, in the land of the living. Now, God, as they stand boldly before Your throne of grace, unafraid to take charge once again of their health—in mind, body, and spirit—reveal to them the path back to a healthy and joy-filled ministry. Reassure them that their work has been and will continue to be "for Your good pleasure." There is no "Plan B." The ministry they are pouring out toward others is also bearing fruit within their hearts. Bless and reassure them now in Christ Jesus, amen.

ENDNOTES

1 2 Corinthians 13:5.

2 K.J. Randall, "Clergy Burnout: Two Different Measures," *Pastoral Psychology* 62 (2013): 335.

3 If you wish to see or take the MBI, especially if you are interested in burnout among populations outside of clergy, you can find it here: https://www.mindgarden.com/117-maslach-burnout-inventory-mbi. I will not be discussing the MBI at length in this book.

4 Two questions, 12 and 14, have been altered slightly to suit any ministry. Dr. Francis' test was created for pastors. I have made these alterations with Dr. Francis' permission.

5 2 Corinthians 13:5.

6 1 Corinthians 10:13.

CHAPTER FOUR

FBI AND INTERVIEW RESPONSES

"Simon, Simon, behold, Satan has demanded permission to sift men like wheat; but I have prayed for you, that your faith may not fail; and you, when you have turned back, strengthen your brothers."[1]

"The Francis Burnout Inventory with its component scales, the Scale of Emotional Exhaustion in Ministry and the Satisfaction in Ministry Scale, can be commended for research among clergy in the fields of work-related psychological health, stress, and burnout."[2]

SELF-PERCEPTION OF BURNOUT

The opening question I asked the chaplains in both iterations of the FBI was not part of the FBI. My goal in asking the question was to set a baseline to understand how well chaplains assessed their burnout both before taking the test for the first time and after we tried to link them with their sending source representatives. Although a few of the ministers wrote in customized responses, for our purpose here, we will limited the results to four possible responses to the statement: I feel drained in fulfilling my ministry roles. The chart below compares the chaplain's self-assessment before taking the first FBI, then three months later after taking the second FBI following intentional attempts to connect with their sending source.

CHAPLAIN'S SELF-ASSESSMENT

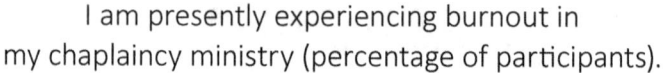

I am presently experiencing burnout in
my chaplaincy ministry (percentage of participants).

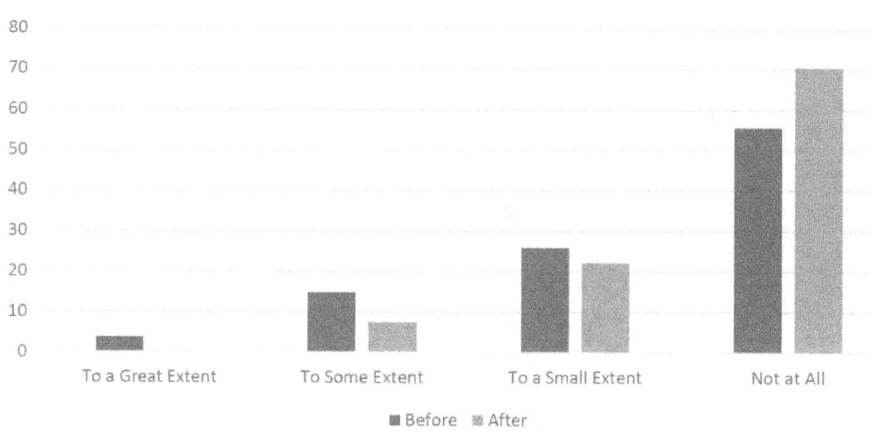

Going into the study, I hypothesized that meetings between chaplains and their pastors would help develop solutions that eased burnout as their relationship grew closer. Another hypothesis was that the conduct of the study itself would elevate awareness of burnout, highlight solutions, and decrease emotional exhaustion while increasing the chaplains' sense of personal accomplishment. The result as represented in this question was an 18.5% improvement toward a perception of eased burnout.

Next we'll look at our participant's responses to the FBI regarding their feelings of professional accomplishment (PA) and emotional exhaustion (EE).

FBI BURNOUT SCORES
27 Chaplain Participants: February 2021

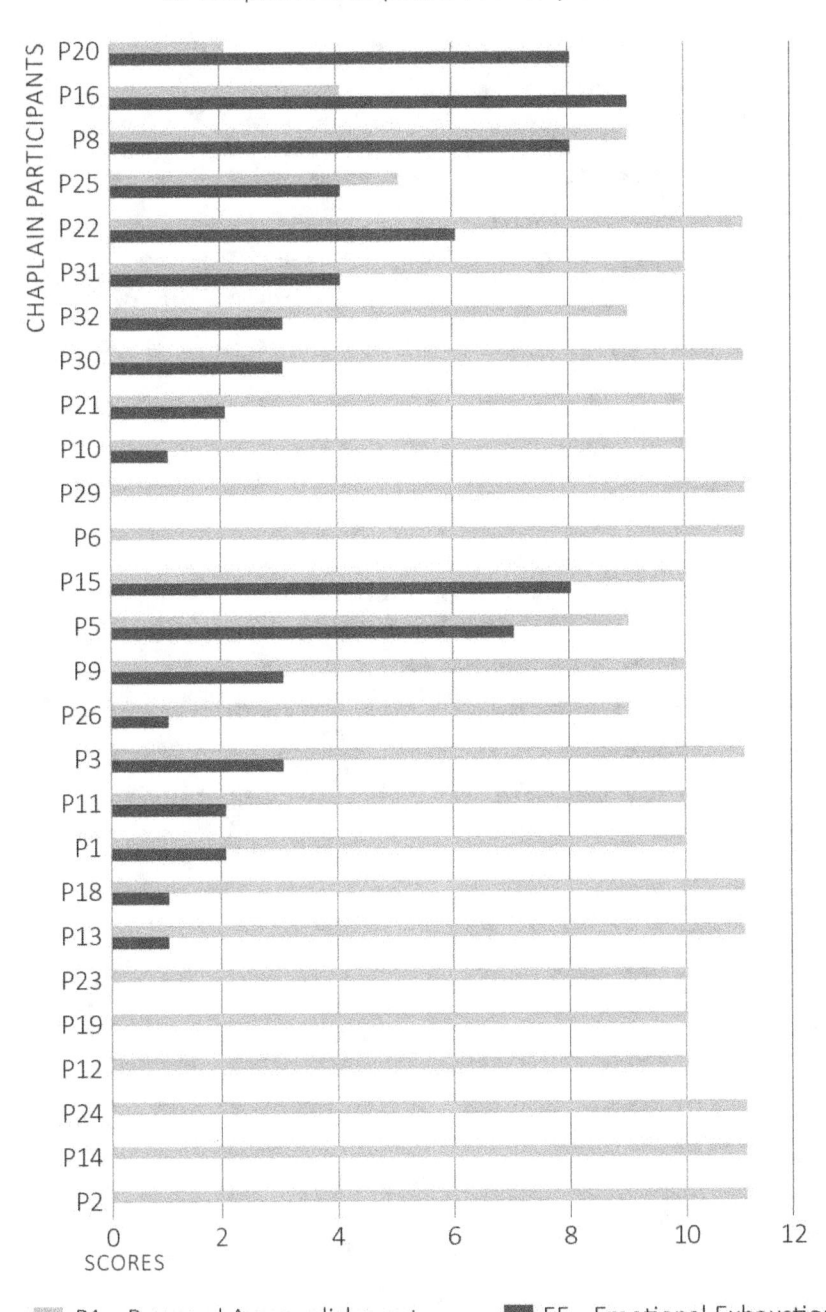

Note: This test was administered *before* any intentional relationship-building was done between chaplains and their sending source.

PA—Personal Accomplishment   EE—Emotional Exhaustion

FBI BURNOUT SCORES
27 Chaplain Participants: April 2021

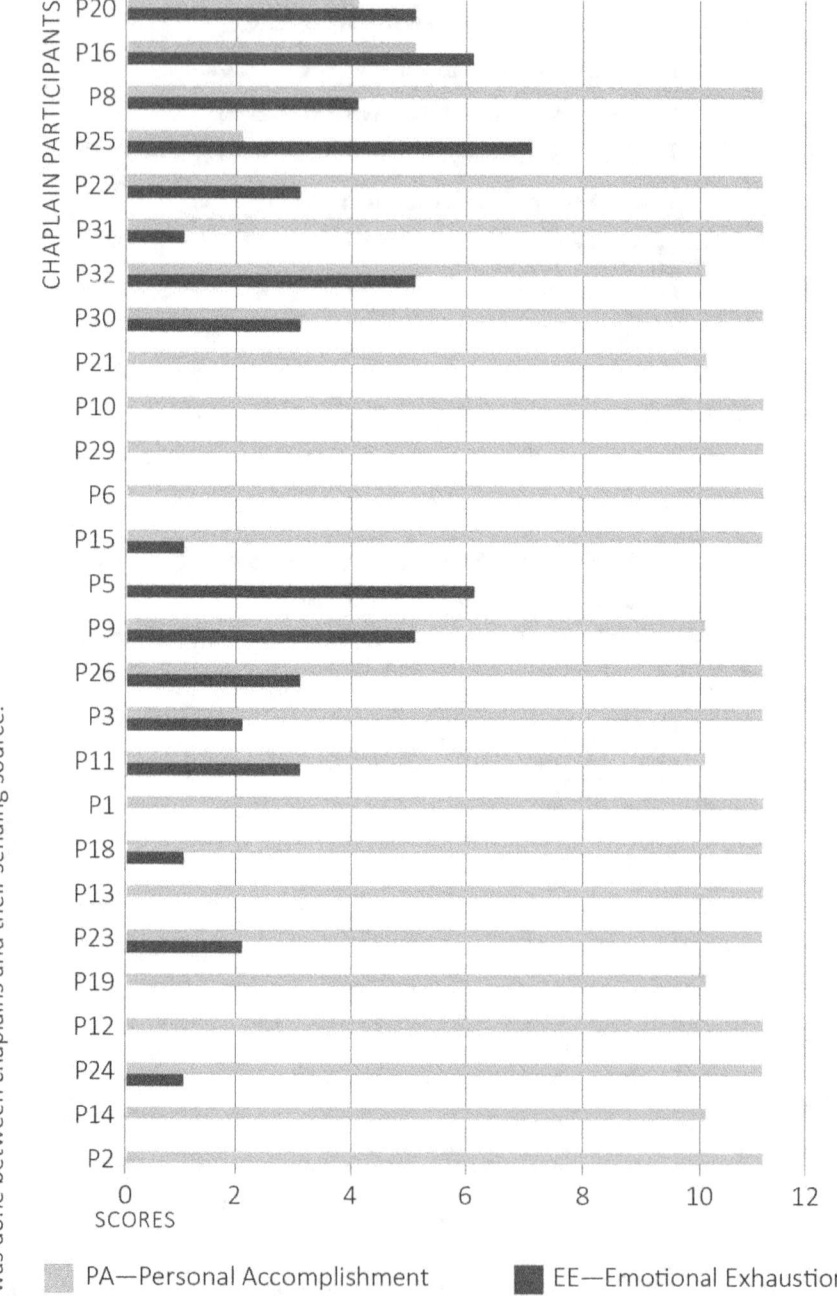

Note: This test was administered *after* intentional relationship-building was done between chaplains and their sending source.

CHAPLAIN PARTICIPANTS

SCORES

PA—Personal Accomplishment   EE—Emotional Exhaustion

RESULTS OF FBI, BEFORE AND AFTER

Each graphic shows the FBI Burnout Scores of our participating chaplains. The first shows their responses to the assessment **before** we worked to link them intentionally with their sending source for support, and the second is taken three months later **after** we attempted to connect each chaplain with their sending source.

Along the bottom of each graph, you see the raw scores (0-11) of each chaplain's response. The chaplain participants are listed vertically on the left, numbered P-1 through P-32.

Here are some things to note from how the chaplains scored:

- Thirty-two chaplains were invited to participate in this study, but only twenty-seven completed the full study. Chaplains kept the number they were originally assigned, noted vertically on the FBI BURNOUT SCORES charts.

- The yellow bar represents each chaplain's feeling of personal accomplishment (PA). The highest possible score was 11.

  - Before taking the FBI, twenty chaplains scored a 10 or an 11 for personal accomplishment (PA). Four scored a 9.

  - If we take out the three low scores, the average "before" result for the sense of personal accomplishment chaplains felt is a 10.25 rating.

  - After taking the FBI, eighteen chaplains scored 11, and six scored ten. Again we removed the three low scores, and the average "after" result increased only to a 10.75.

  - The three low scores remained at 5 points or lower both before and after taking the FBI (P20, P16, P25).

- The blue bar represents each chaplain's assessment of their emotional exhaustion (EE). Again, the highest possible score was 11.

- Before taking the FBI, the average score for emotional exhaustion was 2.8.

- After taking the FBI, the average score for emotional exhaustion shrank to 2.15.

Enough of the statistical analysis—for now. What does this chart mean? In the absence of interview questions, I should explain what the information reveals; it tells us that the study showed a slight increase in the Satisfaction in Ministry Scale and a slight decrease in the Scale of Emotional Exhaustion in Ministry. In simpler terms, generally, there was less blue and more yellow in the *after* at the end of the study, which is good—except for the few chaplains for whom this was not the case.

These positive changes coincided with the participants' self-assessment of the statement: "I am presently experiencing burnout in my chaplaincy ministry," represented in the bar chart on page 58. Their answers revealed their perceptions of their levels of burnout. Overall, they accurately reflected their feelings of burnout compared to what the FBI revealed at both the beginning and the conclusion of the study. If you wish to see pie charts representing the chaplains' answers to all the FBI questions, I have appended them at the back of the book (beginning on page 193). However, I want to share some of the revealing statements the chaplains had to make about their experiences with burnout and with the stressors they faced in the field and in life.

FIRST RESPONDERS

Working with law enforcement and firefighters means working with people who have seen the dark side of life that pastors and other ministers seldom see. The recent political and activist attacks on the law enforcement profession have added an element of stress to their work that has increased their sense of betrayal and decreased their satisfaction in the workplace. That has also spilled over into the firefighter community. Police and firefighters face a greater threat from burnout than just about any other helping profession, according to many studies. Imagine being among the ministers trying to care for those communities.

POLICE AND FIREFIGHTERS FACE A GREATER THREAT FROM BURNOUT THAN JUST ABOUT ANY OTHER HELPING PROFESSION.

Cynicism is common in these professions. Cops face almost daily confrontations with people. Sometimes, those become violent. Even their interactions with ordinary citizens are reminders that their job is often thankless. People don't respond well to receiving traffic tickets. They don't like road closures. They don't like seeing videos of police officers doing what it often takes to arrest the criminals who steal from their stores, sell drugs in their neighborhoods, or break into their homes.

When it happens to them, of course, citizens often want cops to bypass the sometimes slow, difficult legal processes to bring them justice. However, when prosecutors refuse to prosecute the person who stole their car or when legislators decrease sentencing for the vandals in their neighborhood, it isn't the prosecutors or legislators that catch citizens' abuse. When a judge gives a lenient sentence to a murderer, it isn't the court system they yell at. It is the cops on the street who receive their pent-up anger.

In some cities, firefighters wear bullet-proof vests at certain scenes because firefighters get shot, just like cops do. They get yelled at by those whose lives they are trying to save. I've talked with paramedics who have been spit on by homeless people and attacked by overdose victims they've just saved with a dose of Narcan. People often expect firefighters to run into harm's way for them without concern for their own safety. However, they work according to rules meant to ensure their safety as they do their jobs. When people misunderstand those safety measures, they forcefully share their opinions with the firefighters as they work. Cops often joke with their fire department compatriots that they got the job where they are always seen as the hero, but any firefighter can tell you that this is not always the case.

Both professions share many common stressors. They work long shifts. Cops will sometimes work a morning shift for a month, then move to a graveyard shift, and then find themselves working the swing shift. They may finish their eight-hour shift only to be mandated to work another four hours, dashing planned events with family and diminishing their sleep cycle. Firefighters often work twenty-four-hour shifts. After a busy day of training and taking care of the station, the fire engines, and their gear, they may end up running to calls all night long. Their circadian rhythms are a mess, which affects their ability to think clearly in dangerous circumstances. Over time, these random work cycles and disturbed sleep cycles impair their judgment, strain their relationships, and leave them physically, mentally, and emotionally exhausted—not just for a day or a week, but chronically.

Police officers are often exposed to nightmarish incidents, sights, sounds, smells, and confrontations. They go to every homicide and suicide in their cities. They show up at most natural death scenes. They respond to every fatal automobile collision, sometimes handling the dead or mangled victims to assist the coroner or medical examiner. It is bad enough when the victims are adults but so much worse when they are children. Officers deal with drunks, overdosed drug addicts, people with infectious diseases, and the mentally ill. They get assaulted by the people they arrest and by others thinking they are protecting their loved ones who are getting arrested. Their cynicism is well earned. They deal with all the horrifying things that happen daily in society that the average citizen never has to see. Worst of all, they lose partners, friends, and fellow officers or firefighters in the line of duty. And after all of that, they face department administrators, lawyers, and the public, all of whom have days to examine and second-guess their responses to events for which they had only a split second to make a life-or-death decision.

Try reaching that crowd with the "Romans Road" or the "ABCs of Salvation." Their walls are always up. Many have seen the kinds of things that challenge a belief in the existence of God. They *need* to hear about grace and mercy, but they have seen so little of it that it truly sounds like mythology to them. Don't get me wrong, many faithful Christian men and women serve in the fire stations and police precincts across America. I have seen them grow in faith and be a light to others. I have also seen them lose their faith and succumb to the darkness.

These are those of whom Jesus spoke when He said, "I was hungry, and you gave me something to eat; I was thirsty, and you gave me something to drink; I was a stranger, and you invited me in."[3] They hunger and thirst for righteousness but have often become jaded to the point of letting themselves starve on a diet of human cruelty, unable to comprehend the kind of mercy and grace God offers to the world they have experienced. It is exactly this audience to whom Christ has called many chaplains. They need a long drink from the fountain of grace. They are the peacemakers, and they are the sons and daughters of God.

FIRST RESPONDER CHAPLAINS

FIRST RESPONDER CHAPLAINS FACE MANY OF THE SAME STRUGGLES AS COPS AND FIREFIGHTERS.

First responder chaplains face many of the same struggles as cops and firefighters. Chaplains engage a truly incarnate ministry, wearing the uniform, showing up at the calls, working all hours of the day and night, yet trying to empathize with those who are faced daily with humanity's gravest horrors and deepest losses. It is no wonder that chaplains are not immune to the creeping cynicism that prevails among those they serve. One of the study participants stated about this phenomenon:

Everyone I've talked to that has done this job longer than I have—you know, law enforcement, the actual officers, and paramedics and firefighters—we talked about it, and to be honest, there's a kind of cynicism ... I have to consciously tell myself not to respond in the way I am currently thinking ... It's like I'm pretty sure I know all the things that led up to it and the poor choices that were made. I know what's going to happen here and the kind of grief we're going to see, and I have to put on a little bit of a mask to serve that community. It's undeniable that some of that comes from a callous that I'm glad is there. But I have to file that thing away every now and again. I can't let it get too thick ... I have to go back to

Matthew 6 and 7 and realize I'm being all judgy here right now. I don't know this story, and all I know is I see a brother or sister who is suffering and kind of work at that callous a little bit.

The nature of the chaplain's ministry is often hit-and-run. They show up for an hour or two to comfort a family that has lost a loved one, then leave. Often, they never get to find out how that family fares after their consolations are over. One chaplain capsulized this confusing, moment-in-time ministry in this way:

I feel like I do so much so often that it's hard for me to assess. You know? I don't always get feedback. It's like I pop into this person's world, pop into this person's world, pop into this person's world. [I wonder] if I actually do the right thing, did I make a positive difference? I'd like to think so, but I'm not sure if it's effective.

Another chaplain related a different type of frustration they experienced in dealing with their first responders:

It's hard in the chaplain world because there are some things a chaplain can't fix. So, maybe it's effective in the moment, but that person still gives up that career or spirals downhill, and there's not anything I could have done. It always makes you wonder, like, well, did I help at all?

Yet another chaplain discussed the uncertainty of their ministry:

Sometimes it's really clear that I'm getting things done, and at other times—it kind of goes back to my earlier statement about getting into the heads of people—I don't know. I'm not always sure I've done any good in a certain situation.

What you hear in their words are the tell-tale signs of an impaired sense of personal accomplishment. Pastors, missionaries, and other ministers experience the same frustrations. They are never really quite sure if their efforts are having the desired effect. This uncertainty wears on a minister's heart. It eats at the core sense of mission they had when they responded to their calling. Consider this response in one interview from the point of view of a pastor who also worked as a chaplain:

I think the draw on my inner resources as a chaplain can be really deep and fast. Then I get back to my office after a call, and I'm not interested in listening to somebody complain about what someone is saying at church, or a song we sang one Sunday, or which translation of the Bible is the right one. You know, you just kind of want to punch them in the neck at that point. It's like, "Do you realize what just happened two miles down the road? How can you be so professional, so good at your job, and still be such a bunch of junior highers?" Then, with some families in the community, I just want to dad-up on them and wag my finger and go, "If you hadn't ... you wouldn't have wound up here." So, I can feel withdrawn from those I feel called to shepherd. And on any given day, I would trace it back to (the knowledge that) my tank's empty.

Here you start to see the sense of depersonalization that sets in when ministers lose perspective. It's the forest for the trees quandary. Ministers are sometimes so deep in the mess that people create, trying to minister to them in the muck and mire, that they lose compassion and forget the goal of ministry. Some say that the goal is to save souls, to bring the Gospel of Salvation. Ultimately, that is what every pastor, chaplain, evangelist, and missionary would like. After all, what good is it to give them temporary relief from their pain when they are drowning in sin?

However, the goal is the Gospel of the Kingdom—the Good News. The focus is on bringing Heaven to earth, as Jesus taught us to pray: "Your will be done, on earth as it is in Heaven."[4] That goal can become obscured the more time the minister spends with the hurting and the broken. Kingdom ministry takes time. It is plowing ground and sowing seed. Sometimes it is reaping. When we lose the long-term perspective, we don't have as much to give in the short term. The same pastor-chaplain from the quote above pointed out that he had begun "rationing his compassion" in order to cope with the sense of confusion that comes when we are overwhelmed by the immediate needs of the people around us:

WHEN WE LOSE THE LONG-TERM PERSPECTIVE, WE DON'T HAVE AS MUCH TO GIVE IN THE SHORT-TERM.

> *I have to—or it might be that I've chosen to—cope by creating categories. If you're a church person, sorry, you're going to get this, and if you're in this other category, here's what I have available to you. It's all you're going to get because it's what I have available. So, I think maybe I'm going into the bag of clichés a little more often than I did pre-chaplain work. That feels like a decrease in flexibility. Honestly, I would say it's a decrease in being present with that individual—a sort of rationing of compassion.*

Another chaplain noted:

> When that call comes in at 3:00 in the morning, I would not describe myself as enthusiastic. The calls never come at the best time. They seem to come at 3:00 in the morning or 1:00 on Sunday afternoon when my wife and I are settling in to go to a movie together or sitting and watching a football game ... It is certainly easier when the loved one was 95, had just come home from the hospital, and passed.
>
> That's understandable. But the worst one for me was the high school senior who passed away overnight for no known reason. I watched the family just be grilled by Major Crimes and then the Medical Examiner because they considered it a drug problem—and this kid was a 2-sport athlete headed to college.

As I noted before, studies have shown that pastors tend to have a very resilient response to the stressors of ministry. This is often attributed to their sense of calling, the unique knowledge that they entered into their helping profession because God had called them to it. He equips the called. As I have shown, they still experience the emotionally exhausting aspects of helping people. Yet, their outlook often defies the constant disappointments and the feelings they face that they may be working on that treadmill and still getting nowhere. The saving grace is their ability to see the wide-open fields of harvest Jesus referred to, knowing that God's Word will never return void. One minister described it like this:

> I was [just] sitting in the office with my senior pastor, and we were crying. We weren't talking about any one particular

situation but the astounding amount of grief that is underway. I happen to be the kind of person who tends to feel it. So, the reason I answered [the question] that way is that I am deeply saddened, and I feel an increasing pressure and a weight at the same time.

God's faithfulness is rising. I mean, it's the promise of the New Testament. It's so faith-building that God is just so present. And so, there's a joy that's unexplainable, the presence of Christ is matching and exceeding—that there's a new understanding of what I think Jesus meant by abundant life. It doesn't mean more money and a bigger house. It means you're going to cry more often, but you're going to laugh more often. I didn't want to say, "Everything's great!" because it's not, and I feel the pressure. I don't know what the outcome is going to be, but at the same time, I feel like God's faithfulness is, in a sense, matching it and kind of pulling us along through it.

Enthusiasm for the work is often hard to come by, as many chaplains noted that it wasn't always easy to get up for the typical, untimely call of a deceased person and a family waiting in grief:

There are some days that phone rings and I'm like, are you kidding me? I have to sit with another dead body for three hours? I wanted to make cookies.

One chaplain called himself a "seed planter." He stated that chaplaincy was not a ministry like evangelism, where there are visible responses to the message of the Gospel. Rather, he says:

I know what my role is. To bring Christ to a world that is fallen and broken, and how we're called by God to go out and share that with others.

That sense of mission is sometimes bolstered by a chance meeting with people the chaplain had ministered to in their darkest hour:

There have been times that I have gone out and ministered on a call and said, "Did I do any good?" And then, the funny thing is that I'll meet that person maybe a year later, and they'll say, "Oh, I'm so glad you were there. You have no idea how you ministered to me." And yet, my own personal assessment of my effectiveness on that call was quite the opposite. So, it's easy to say you're not certain [about the effectiveness of your ministry] because you can't truly get inside the head and heart of the individual you're ministering to.

Despite the challenges of first responder chaplaincy, twenty-four of the twenty-seven participants agreed or strongly agreed with the statement, "I gain a lot of personal satisfaction from fulfilling my ministry roles." One chaplain captured the intangible nature of ministry that is hard to quantify in a study yet drives the high job satisfaction that many clergy share about their ministry experience:

You know, there is a countervailing element that continues to regenerate me and keep me focused and purposed. Have you ever heard of the theology of blessings for obedience? The Reader's Digest version of that is that if you are true and purposefully obedient to the call of God, the Lord will be faithful to come alongside you, regenerate you, give you a sense of purpose, and give you a sense of joy in the work that you do. And that is one of the primary blessings of obedience. It's the Holy Spirit regenerating our spirit. That's a huge thing. It keeps me focused. It keeps me committed, and it gives me joy in the work that I do.

A sense of high personal accomplishment can erode over the course of ministry. If pastors, chaplains, and other ministers are not intentional in their self-care practices, they may ultimately face deep discouragement. If they are already running on that treadmill, emotionally exhausted and growing in cynicism, a steady decrease of awareness of the good they are doing can send them spiraling into burnout. Burnout takes time to set in. It is easy to get so busy in the work of ministry that we start to work out of our own strength rather than relying on the Spirit—and heeding the protective limitations God has placed upon us. How, then, can a man or woman of God plan to avoid burnout?

IF PASTORS, CHAPLAINS, AND OTHER MINISTERS ARE NOT INTENTIONAL IN THEIR SELF-CARE PRACTICES, THEY MAY ULTIMATELY FACE DEEP DISCOURAGEMENT.

REFLECTION

We live in the tension of the *already* and the *not yet*: Gerhardus Vos' concept of the *already—not yet*. This creates a paradox for us in ministry. The Kingdom is in you, yet it is still coming. We work within a mystery. When we don't *see* the results *now*, we tend to forget that there is still a *not yet*. Thus, our expectations are seldom met, and disappointment follows. We are unable to see the effects of our ministrations because we often become stuck on one side of the *already—not yet* equation.

> *"Not that I have already obtained it, or have already become*
> *perfect, but I press on in order that I may lay hold of that*
> *for which also I was laid hold of by Christ Jesus. Brethren,*
> *I do not regard myself as having laid hold of it yet; but*
> *one thing I do: forgetting what lies behind and reaching*
> *forward to what lies ahead, I press on toward the goal*
> *for the prize of the upward call of God in Christ Jesus."*
> PHILIPPIANS 3:12-14

We have not already obtained it—the resurrection from the dead. And yet it is ours. We are not yet perfected, but we already possess perfection. John tells us we are *now* God's children, but what we will be has not yet been seen.[5] Paul tells us that we are seated with Christ in Heaven[6], but who feels the glory of that exalted position continually? The writer of Hebrews tells us that everything has been put into subjection to Jesus, yet we do not see everything in subjection to Him presently.[7]

Reflect for a moment with the God "who gives life to the dead and calls into being things that do not exist"[8] on your ministry's unseen impact.

- What helps you patiently endure when you cannot yet see the results of your labor?

- Recall how you felt when you first answered God's call. What made you excited to serve Him in this way?

- Pause and consider the tension between *already* and *not yet*. Can you accept what is *already* true of and for you, even while you do *not yet* see it?

- How do you experience the blessing of Holy Spirit regeneration within your spirit? What will it take to *forget what lies behind* and reach forward to *take hold of it*?

PRAYER OF ENCOURAGEMENT

God, I thank You for this minister showing up in the earth as the tangible expression of Christ. They are Your hands and feet. With Your help, they comfort the brokenhearted; bind their wounds, and bring others a cup of cold water in Jesus' name. You have called them. You have set them apart. You have taken notice of every act of service to You, and their obedience brings You joy. Bring them into Your mystery and give them a glimpse of the already, even that which is not yet. Renew their spirit today and fill them with fresh joy. In Christ Jesus, amen.

ENDNOTES

1   Luke 22:31-32.

2   K.J. Randall, "Clergy Burnout: Two Different Measures," *Pastoral Psychol* 62 (2013):339.

3   Matthew 25:35.

4   Matthew 6:10.

5   1 John 3:2.

6   Ephesians 2:6.

7   See Hebrews 2:8-9.

8   Romans 4:17.

"I KNOW WHAT MY ROLE IS—TO
BRING CHRIST TO A WORLD THAT
IS FALLEN AND BROKEN, AND HOW
WE'RE CALLED BY GOD TO GO OUT
AND SHARE THAT WITH OTHERS."

—A CHAPLAIN FROM MY STUDY

CHAPTER FIVE

MINISTRY ON THE TREADMILL

"But prove yourselves doers of the word, and not just hearers who deceive themselves. For if anyone is a hearer of the word and not a doer, he is like a man who looks at his natural face in a mirror; for once he has looked at himself and gone away, he has immediately forgotten what kind of person he was. But one who has looked intently at the perfect law, the law of freedom, and has continued in it, not having become a forgetful hearer but an active doer, this person will be blessed in what he does."[1]

"Spaite (1999) suggested that pastors are vulnerable to developing a Messiah complex, or the self-denial of one's legitimate needs in favor of saving or rescuing others, which may result in emotional insulation and isolation."[2]

SUMMARIZING BURNOUT

To keep in mind what we are fighting against so we can continue to fight the good fight, let's look at burnout again. Ministry burnout can happen over time as we expend compassion for others, become exhausted, and begin to distance ourselves from God and those we serve. We then lose our sense that we are serving a meaningful and productive purpose. We overextend ourselves—that is the nature of ministry. When we say "yes" to too many needs, we will become exhausted.

If you haven't yet watched *The Chosen*, I highly recommend it. This television series provides cultural and life context to many Scriptures we have often read without knowing what it would have been like to live alongside Jesus in His ministry. While some consider it "adding to Scripture," I have enjoyed how it fills in gaps in my ability to visualize the relationships and daily interactions between Jesus, His disciples, and other characters we meet briefly in reading the Bible.

In season 2, episode 3, entitled "Matthew 4:24," we see a day in the life of the disciples as they prepare for Jesus' *Sermon on the Mount*, even as Jesus is employed with the business described in the passage for which the episode is named: "And the news about Him spread throughout Syria; and they brought to Him all who were ill, those suffering with various diseases and severe pain, demon-possessed, people with epilepsy, and people who were paralyzed; and He healed them."

The end of the episode shows us something not found in Scripture. We see Jesus completely spent after the day's ministry. It's not something we are taught to think about, as if Jesus were not all God *and* all man. I normally pictured Jesus just moving about His healing and teaching ministry, full of strength and vitality, never suffering from the kind of exhaustion our physical bodies and minds encounter after a long, hard day at work. Like me, you may presume that Jesus was only doing what

His Father was doing,[3] and that this automatically implies that He never got tired. However, Scripture records that He slept in the boat during the storm as the disciples fought the waves. He often retreated alone to "a quiet place" or "the wilderness," and He prayed—sweating blood—through a most trying time at Gethsemane.

In Philippians 2:7, we are told that "He emptied himself," a term often referred to as the *kenosis*, wherein Jesus accepted limitations to His divinity in order to conduct Himself on earth as a man. In my own theology, this means Jesus literally set aside His *God-ness* to become a man. Several reasons attach to this startling act of God becoming incarnate, or taking on the flesh, and being "God tabernacled with us."

Many theologians greater than I have attempted to explain this, so please don't declare me a heretic if I don't express it perfectly. When Jesus set aside His divinity, He accepted the same limitations you and I face as we walk through this life in the flesh:

- He faced hunger and thirst.
- He needed to grow (even through the awkwardness of puberty) from childhood to adulthood.
- He bore the limitations of time and space (He had to walk everywhere and could not be omnipresent).
- He endured temptation.
- He depended upon His Heavenly Father for knowledge and guidance.

Jesus emptied Himself that He might be able to place the perfect sacrifice on the Cross—a sinless human being—to be a sacrifice for all human beings. We must not fall into the Docetic trap of believing that Jesus, as God, could not suffer or be tempted to sin and therefore only *appeared* to be going through life in human form. Neither should we fall into the Gnostic trap on the other side by believing that Jesus was merely an enlightened man.

Jesus was fully God, having chosen to allow the limitations of our flesh upon Himself on His way to the Cross. It was an act of God's will to make His Son fully man, to tabernacle with us, and thus to show Himself to be the only means by which we might find forgiveness of our sins and come into right relationship with Him.

This self-limitation of God to save His created ones—you and me—is one of the great distinctions of our faith; one that is both utterly unique among the claims of all religions and the greatest proof that Jesus is, indeed, the Messiah. Therefore, He is the way, the truth, and the life for all. Mankind has never had the capacity to save himself, each of us having sinned and fallen short of God's glory. God did not put on a puppet show to fool us into thinking He became a man, dying in a mock act of self-sacrifice that would become a mere symbol of a generalized salvation; and one with no real effect.

He emptied Himself of His divine attributes so you and I might know a very real God who so identified with His creation that He became our substitute on the Cross, the spotless lamb for sinners slain, astounding the rulers and authorities in the heavenly realms by offering us the free gift of a very real salvation. It was a righteous act that only God could perform and that only a sinless man could satisfy.

With such limitations, therefore, it is not a stretch to assume that Jesus likely faced exhaustion during the course of daily ministry. Pastors who have spent all Sunday morning putting the final touches on their sermons, setting up for church, greeting congregants as they arrive, administering the service and giving their message, praying for people, shaking hands as they depart, and then spooling up for the Sunday evening service know exhaustion. Pastors who have had the privilege of engaging in daily revival services or running week-long conferences know fatigue. Any minister who has spent a day of concerted effort in prayer, prophetic ministry, teaching, or counseling knows exhaustion. Even knowing what to say or do because we are so in tune with what the Father is saying or doing does not exempt us from our human limitations. When we pour out, we become spent.

With thousands pressing Jesus for more teaching, concerned loved ones bringing their sick and demonically possessed before Him by the thousands, and the occasional need to feed them all with nothing but a basket of bread and fish, Jesus very likely faced a physical and emotional drain at the end of most days. The episode of *The Chosen* I have referenced captured that well, with Jesus returning to His tent late at night, barely able to walk, in need of the ministrations of His followers. If He ultimately became obedient unto death, why should we not assume that He was also obedient unto exhaustion? After all, exhaustion is not a sin.

But that is part of our problem, at times. We equate exhaustion with a sort of sin of inadequacy. We then build our schedules to bring ourselves to the brink of exhaustion every day, refusing to say "no" because we are convinced things will fall apart if we do not engage, and too busy to hear God tell us, "No." Then, we refuse to admit that we are indeed depleted, fatigued, tired, sore, or spent. We get up and do it all over, day after day, week after week, never counting the long-term cost of the repeated insults to our bodies, minds, and spirits.

WE EQUATE EXHAUSTION WITH A SORT OF SIN OF INADEQUACY.

Even when we take a vacation, we don't rest. We joke once it is over that we need a vacation to recover from our vacation. We spend less time in prayer because of the needs of the day and then pretend that God will give us the strength to endure when we find ourselves seldom returning to Him for that very strength. It is no wonder that we ultimately lose the capacity for ministering to other humans when we finally begin to resent the fact that they are the reason for our exhaustion!

In truth, however, they are not the reason. Let's look at some symptoms of emotional exhaustion. You can find these anywhere on the internet, but I have gathered some specific to the ministerial context.

1. You have no enthusiasm for the coming day of ministry or the next call-out.

2. You cannot see taking another counseling appointment.

3. When you pray for others, it feels empty, shallow, and scripturally vague.

4. You tell people you will pray for them rather than praying on the spot. Then you don't.

5. You can no longer feel real empathy for the problems of others.

6. Your sermons or lessons tread over the same old ground because it is easier than trying to hear what the Father is speaking now.

7. You spend far more time on social media, television, video games, or other distractions than on planning and preparing for ministry.

8. When you are supposed to be engaged with people at coffee or over dinner, you find yourself easily distracted by your phone.

9. You *listen* to people, but you don't *hear* them.

10. Your office becomes your prison. You seldom leave because you might run into people.

11. It is hard to feel that your ministry is having an impact, often leading to shorter days at work or doing ministry.

12. You complain. Often. About everything.

13. You don't hear God's voice as often or at all.

14. Every suggestion for how to improve ministry is taken as a criticism, and every new criticism becomes a crushing blow.

15. You find yourself angry, frustrated, alone, irritable, and deeply disappointed. Sometimes you cannot even put a finger on the object of these feelings.

16. It becomes easy to blame others.

17. You see your relationships suffering but feel helpless to do anything about it.

18. You may struggle with depression or anxiety—or both.

There are many more possible symptoms, and while most are common to all, some are unique to you. Your personality and giftings may create a whole set of unique symptoms. The extrovert may become much more introverted, which depletes them. The introvert may spend all of their time alone, and that isolation becomes dangerous. The one who teaches may lose their passion for teaching, while the one who writes may suffer from chronic writer's block. The prophetic personality may become an angry, fire-summoning prophet, rather than meting out prophetic ministry for edification, exhortation, and consolation. The leader may demand respect rather than commanding it. The server may stop serving because they feel no one notices or appreciates their service.

No matter what the symptoms, the effects of exhaustion kill outreach and creativity. When you have nothing in your cup, it is hard to overflow.

The leap from exhaustion to depersonalization is a small one. This is where you disconnect from other people as ends in and of themselves, treating them instead as means to, or as intrusive distractions from, the end of your own peace of mind. In other words, you retreat into a defensive posture, protecting yourself from those God has called you to serve. The depersonalizing minister becomes a toxic leader and begins to injure the very people they love.

Let us summarize some symptoms of depersonalization, once again tailored to the ministry context. Many of these are extensions of emotional exhaustion and clearly overlap the symptoms of exhaustion.

1. A marked decrease in your devotional life—prayer, worship, and Bible study. You feel distant from God and His Word.

2. You become angry at people. "Ministry would be great if it wasn't for the people."

3. You fear people. You don't approach them, and you fear being approached.

4. People have too many problems and won't heed your counsel or teaching.

5. People become objects to be judged rather than those you were called to reach.

6. You know more than others. You are always right.

7. It is easier to focus on theology, philosophy, and abstract ideas than on being with people.

8. God feels more like your judge than your Father.

9. God's goodness feels like an abstract concept.

10. God is good to others, but not to you.

11. You are tempted to resign in frustration and move away from the heartache.

12. You are cynical about every new idea, every new move of God, every story of someone else's miracle or victory.

13. You question your calling.

14. You may question your faith.

15. You don't act on your giftings as often—or at all.

16. You cannot see how God is using you; therefore, you may be angry at how He is using you. (Consider Jonah.)

17. Scripture becomes a defense for your attitudes rather than a challenge to them.

18. You may suffer from bitterness and unforgiveness.

This list is not exhaustive, and I am sorry if some of these hit home; if they do, you may be experiencing burnout. I struggled writing these lists, as many of them do hit home for me. You may not even be willing, presently, to admit to many of these symptoms. You do, however, see their effects on your ministry. Perhaps you may even be experiencing some physical symptoms, which I will now list. Remember, we are made in God's image. We are mind and body and spirit. What impacts any one facet of our being impacts all facets. See if you recognize yourself in any of these:

1. Headaches or migraines

2. Sleep disturbances or sleep that is not refreshing, sleep apnea

3. Grinding your teeth/clenching your jaw

4. Increase in blood pressure, perhaps even hypertension, heart palpitations

5. Muscle tension or joint pain

6. Eating disorders—overeating or missing meals

7. Digestive tract disorders or ulcers

8. Anxiety or panic attacks

9. Restlessness, inability to be physically calm

10. Self-medication, either with drugs or alcohol

11. Reduced physical fitness activities or abilities

12. Bodily weariness

13. Brain fog, forgetfulness, lack of focus or concentration

14. Reduced resistance to colds, flu, allergies, or other illnesses

This list is also not comprehensive. However, many of these are common physical symptoms of burnout. We don't come by all of these symptoms naturally. While many result from stress, heightened symptomology may result from the levels and duration of stress that can lead to burnout. Never accept the idea that you are "just getting older" as an excuse for being sick or run down. Even if you're not like me and believe that when rightly related to God, we can walk in perfect health, certainly you may agree with me that it is not God's design that we should suffer in increasing measure as we pour ourselves out in ministry. Some suffering is self-imposed. I would suggest that we learn the difference

WE MUST LEARN THE DIFFERENCE BETWEEN SUFFERING FOR THE CROSS AND SUFFERING BECAUSE OF OUR FAILURE TO HEAR GOD'S VOICE WHEN HE BIDS US BE STILL.

between suffering for the Cross and suffering because of our failure to hear God's voice when He bids us be still.

REMEMBERING OUR LIMITATIONS

We have physical, mental, emotional, and spiritual limitations. God did not design you to *do* all things; otherwise, He would have just made you and not the whole Church. Jesus accepted limitations, and so should we. His capacity for ministry was tied entirely to His relationship with His Father. Your capacity is limited by your lack of relationship with the Father. However, it can also be expanded with more intimate time with Him. This does not mean you will be able to do all things for all people, but it does mean that you will have the strength to do exactly what you see the Father doing and say what you hear Him saying. Like Jesus, when you work within your limitations, you can accomplish all things the Father sent you to do.

One of my research participants was extremely driven. He showed a moderately high burnout rate in his FBI score. He works in the medical field and has a degree that required years of study. While working in the clinic, he decided to take up ministerial studies and started a Master of Theology program. He also entered chaplaincy for his local fire department. Even I thought that was crazy. I admired it, but really, that is a lot to take on. He had recently moved to another city and was not yet linked in with his church leadership, as COVID had limited their meetings during his move. I'll discuss later the importance of chaplains being linked to church leaders, but just the fact that he had an overwhelming schedule was enough for me to see the reasons for his burnout scores.

Another participant also had limited connections to her church and pastor but took on chaplaincy in a large, metropolitan police department with a high call volume. She had little formal training, and no schooling focused on ministry. She had previously worked in a hospital as a chaplain and had suffered an incident that left her with PTSD. She then faced another series of traumas with the police department, including one that challenged her capacity to minister to police officers. Sadly, the overwhelming workload, the lack of training, and the compounding traumas caused her to leave chaplaincy in anger and frustration.

Your ministry is not the only thing going on in your life—or at least, it shouldn't be. The constant needs of others in your life outside of your ministry can drain your resources, as well, taking away from what you have to give to your church or outreach efforts. A chaplain who had previously suffered burnout shared this:

> It's never just chaplaincy. It's your whole life that plays in together. At least that's what went into my burnout before ... it wasn't just the heavy load that I was taking at that time. I was doing anywhere from 20 to 30 death calls a month, you know, a huge load, and there would be days when I'd maybe take two or three (death calls) in a day. But then there's the family, and there's all the things that go into your other life.

Whether it is overloading your plate with work, paying attention to the needs of your spouse or children, taking on extra education, or starting out with little training or education, you are limited in time and space. You cannot be everywhere at once, and you cannot do everything that people demand of you. Let's look at how Jesus did it. He didn't just limit His Godhood. He had other healthy boundaries in place:

- He limited who had access to Him.

- He limited when and how He did ministry.

- He limited where He chose to go.

- He guarded His time with His Father.

- He didn't take all His disciples into every event in His life.
- He put off His family at some times and brought them into His life at others.

His plan wasn't random. It was formed daily in the presence of His Father. He limited Himself by making choices—choosing what He would and would not do each day.

Jesus chose to be limited in His incarnation to show us how we might be rightly related to God the Father—and thereby able to perform all of the deeds He commanded us to do as we align ourselves with Father God. He revealed what a righteous human being could do, creating an effective ministry while staying within the bounds of His chosen human constraints.

It might be said that because of what He chose *not to do,* He became the most effective and powerful minister in history. He chose the *right thing*, not just the next thing. He remained Spirit-guided, whereas we often are guided by the tyranny of the urgent. He kept focus by keeping His relationship with the Father first, the constant urging of the Spirit next, and the mission for which He came third. People can get in the way of all three if we let them. For Jesus, all three were in perfect agreement. But they arose from His *being*, not from an incessant need for *doing*. Jesus demonstrated green pastureland ministry and eschewed the treadmill.

> **JESUS KEPT FOCUS BY KEEPING HIS RELATIONSHIP WITH THE FATHER FIRST, THE CONSTANT URGING OF THE SPIRIT NEXT, AND THE MISSION FOR WHICH HE CAME THIRD.**

I believe we are all called to perform all of the ministries Jesus commanded—not all of us to every ministry, but all of us capable of the unique ministries to which God has equipped and called us individually. As the Church universal, we heal the sick, raise the dead, cleanse the lepers, and cast out demons. We go to the nations, baptize, and teach. We preach the Kingdom of God and of Heaven. We love one another. We are even told to do greater works than He did.[4] Name your miracle, or your sermon, or your command of natural forces, or your prophetic utterance, or your wise counsel, or your compassionate act of love: I believe Jesus wants us to do greater things, just as He said. He never put a caveat on that. He only said we would be able because He goes to the Father.

Your experience of limitation does not limit His Word. However, you are limited by the same factors He permitted in Himself. You are human. You have a physical body and cannot be omnipresent. You don't know all things, but you can know what you need to know for every deed He has called you to perform. You have finite powers, but you can summon the God who moves mountains. It all depends upon the act of your will that puts you in His throne room daily, and it requires your obedience to His voice. Jesus limited Himself so we could see a righteous life lived in absolute obedience to and dependence upon the Father.

If God did not tell Jesus to do everything, I am guessing He won't tell you to take on everything, either. If God did not send Jesus to everyone—though He sent Jesus *for* everyone—He is probably not sending you to everyone, either. What is important is limiting yourself and knowing your limitations. Only do what you see the Father doing and only speak what you hear Him speaking. If you are not seeing what He is doing or hearing what He is saying, that might be a clue that you need to stop what you are doing and saying. Stop, look, and listen. Then obey. Anything else you add may well be your first step toward burnout. It is a trustworthy saying that we should stop asking God to bless what we are doing and instead do what He is blessing. Working in your own strength fences in the pastureland and puts you on the treadmill. You can do nothing on your own.

REFLECTION

The temptation of ministry is to try to do all things. After all, Paul said we are to be all things to all men, right?

> *"I can do all things through Him who strengthens me."*
> PHILIPPIANS 4:13

You can't do all things. You can only do all things *in Him*. Jesus acknowledged and embraced the limitations of humanity. Even He could do nothing on His own, but only what He saw His Father doing, and He did those things in the same way in which He saw His Father doing them. His imperative was that He should and could only do those things He saw His Father doing—those things the Father was blessing.

It is wise to follow Jesus' example here. We, too, are limited. Take a moment to reflect on the ministries, appointments, programs, committees, and commitments you have taken on.

- Prayerfully consider which of those things you have taken the time to see the Father doing. List them out.

- Which ones have you taken on without consulting with the Father?

- What now will you do about these things?

PRAYER OF ENCOURAGEMENT

Father, I thank You for sending Your Son, Jesus, to take on our flesh and become that perfect sacrifice so I could be forgiven and restored to right relationship with You. I repent now for everything I have tried to do in my own strength, regardless of how pure I may have thought my motives to be, but taken on without pausing to sense Your voice and heed Your guidance. I am tired. My weariness has pulled me further from You.

Bring me back. Help me to pause in green pastures and beside still waters until my soul is restored and my cup runneth over once again. Restore the joy of my salvation, and teach me how to rest. I step off the ministry treadmill today, trusting that Your plans for me are good and my purpose from You is possible. I place my exhausted soul into Thy tender care, trusting that You will make me whole again. In Christ Jesus, amen.

ENDNOTES
1 James 1:22-25.

2 Diane J. Chandler, "Pastoral Burnout and the Impact of Personal Spiritual Renewal, Rest-taking, and Support System Practices," *Pastoral Psychology* 58 (Dec. 2008): 274

3 See John 5:19 – "Truly, truly, I say to you, the Son can do nothing of Himself, unless it is something He sees the Father doing; for whatever the Father does, these things the Son also does in the same way."

4 Matthew 10:8; Matthew 28:19; Matthew 10:7; Luke 9:2,60; John 13:34; John 14:12.

CHAPTER SIX

SEEKING THE PASTURELAND

"I am the door; if anyone enters through Me, he will be saved, and will go in and out and find pasture."[1]

"Some clergy appear to drive themselves so relentlessly that they experience adrenaline withdrawal symptoms (restlessness, fatigue, irritability) when they attempt to rest or take vacations."[2]

HOW DO I GET OFF THE TREADMILL?

If you are still reading, it is likely because you have courageously admitted you are somewhere in the cycle of burnout or someone you care about is struggling with it, and you seek to better understand how to help them. Perhaps something I've written has struck you and caused you to start the process of repentance. Burnout is a sin, like any other sin. It has caused a separation between you and God. It isn't murder, divorce, or adultery—although burnout can lead to any of those. Any time we are not in right relationship with the Father, we are in sin.

If you don't believe me, just ask Uzzah.[3] Uzzah missed the instructions on how to move the Ark of the Covenant, though he was a priest of Israel. Moving the Ark was no small matter, and Uzzah should have paid careful attention to how it was to be moved. He was crushed by the Ark when it fell. I know. It's a harsh story, but don't we do the same when we get into a cycle of not listening to the Father, doing only what He does, and saying only what He says? Some call it the sin of presumption. We presume we are doing His work when in reality, we are doing work almost entirely of our own making. That kind of work will crush you.

It is time to repent.

You must entertain a *different pattern of thinking*.

And it must be God-led.

"But," I hear you ask, "how do I think along with God when I cannot even hear His voice? And I wouldn't trust my hearing even if He spoke to me now!"

Thankfully, God works in His sons and daughters quite differently today than in Uzzah's time. There is no immediate death penalty for touching the Ark.

However, if you persist in your burnout pattern of behavior, you may develop further medical, marital, and psychological issues that could take your life sooner than you were meant to go. Heart disease is no simple matter, and neither are affairs of the heart. An anxious heart is not God's will for you. Burnout is most certainly about your heart—the wellspring of life that you are to guard above all things.[4] The heart is the wellspring of life. If you squeeze it hard enough, its flow will decrease. Squeeze it long enough, and it will cease flowing entirely.

AN ANXIOUS HEART IS NOT GOD'S WILL FOR YOU.

As you confront burnout, you get to decide: Will it be fight or flight?

Understand that sometimes flight is good. There is a reason why God equipped us with both these instincts. Sometimes we can hold onto a ministry, a church, a location, or a people for so long that we have no idea that God has been telling us it is time to move on. You don't want to be in the position of fleeing from something, but toward something. God's mercies are new every morning, and His plans are bigger than your ability to mess them up. He will let you catch up to the position you were already supposed to have attained.

However, God may call you to stand your ground and fight. You can fix the toxic practices and patterns of thinking *and* get off the treadmill without walking away from the ministry defeated. You don't necessarily have to leave the church, ministry, city, or state to which you feel called. Standing your ground is an option that requires some serious soul-searching in God's presence. Fighting means you will need energy to expend. Remember what we have already discussed: You can do nothing on your own, that is, without God. It takes humility to realize how lost you have become while burning out. It takes discipline to get off the treadmill and adopt a new pace that will help you remain healthy in your ministry.

No book can tell you which one is the right call for you. That is entirely between you and God. Sometimes He will give hints about what to do through your spouse, children, church board, trusted advisor, or perhaps a miraculous event. Don't wait so long that those hints show up as divorce papers, truancy notices, pink slips, or a car accident. Taking no action may well cause God to shout. As C.S. Lewis observed, "... pain insists upon being attended to. God whispers to us in our pleasures, speaks in our conscience, but shouts in our pains: it is His megaphone to rouse a deaf world."[5]

Beginning a thing is often the hardest part. When deeply entrenched in a pattern, breaking free from the cycle can seem overwhelming. Start with small course corrections. The first correction should be bolstering your time with God. Get alone with Him and tell Him where you are in your head and your heart. If a simple story of a prodigal returning home ends with a father giving his wayward son royal robes, a signet ring, and fine sandals, how much more will be the restoration of a good Heavenly Father for His servants in ministry? He will always entertain His sons and daughters in His courts. Take time to fast and seek an audience with God. Get into His throne room. Get real before Him and get real with yourself. Let God begin the pruning process as you pray and worship.

In my lowest times during burnout, worship was always a holy place. At times it was the only place where I knew He had not forsaken me. If that is the only thing He tells you to do for the rest of your life, obey. It is the only place where you will be able to un-yoke yourself from those burdens. He will eventually replace your burdens with His—the yoke that is easy and the burden that is light. Until then, just get in His presence. There are no answers anywhere else. One day in His courts is better than a thousand elsewhere. I had forgotten that, and perhaps you have forgotten that, too.

Abba may take His time with you there. Don't rush. Don't be in a hurry. Will Reagan and United Pursuit have a song called "Not in a Hurry" that deeply encouraged me in my first awkward steps off the treadmill. I encourage you to find it and listen.[6]

Stay in that place with God until you can feel the soft grass beneath your feet again. Let your legs rest. Enjoy His presence and remain there until He says to go out again. It may require many days of concerted time in His presence. It may take weeks away from the work that you've built into your life. It may take years. He will repay the years the locusts have eaten.[7] No ministry (or minister) can survive without His presence, so don't be in a hurry.

NO MINISTRY (OR MINISTER) CAN SURVIVE WITHOUT HIS PRESENCE.

Become a worshiper again. Become a child. Let the Father take your rags and your rage and fit you instead with a robe and His peace. He has not left you. He has not forsaken you. He is happy to have you back. God did not build you for the treadmill of church growth or educational overload or busy schedules or saving the world all over again. Abide in His presence until you hear His voice again. Once you are renewed as a tabla rasa—a clean slate—let Him write His vision on your heart. Be willing to put aside every ambition you have built in your striving and await His instructions. Then, simply obey.

BUILDING HEALTHY HABITS

At the risk of sounding like I know what you must do next, I will venture some wisdom for creating healthier habits for your ministry that will help you be a faithful *doer* of the Word. Don't assume God is just refitting you for the run from which you just about collapsed. He may begin telling you the things you need to clear from your schedule, the things you were doing that were not His plans but yours. It may require disappointing some people because you have to say no—possibly to something to which you have already given your "yes."

It is possible that God is telling you to stop what you are doing. Maybe He will ask you to leave your church or police department or hospital ministry. They were never yours to begin with, so let them go if He bids you to let them go. He won't tell you to leave your family, but perhaps He wants to change the rhythms of your family life. You might have to disappoint your kids by altering sports schedules, school programs, or media input. He may tell you to drop everything and go to school, find a place in the mission field, or focus on a non-ministry job. More than likely, He will start with just one thing.

Do that one thing.

Do it until He gives you another.

If you want to heal—and avoid future burnout crashes—don't add anything until God moves. Do only what you see Him doing.

STEWARD YOUR HEALTH

As you wait on Him, you can start living in a manner that better stewards your health. Stop rushing around so much that you don't eat or are eating fast food so you can get to the next thing on your schedule. Make your diet a very real and studied effort. Healthy eating is one of the first things to go for many who start down the path toward burnout. Eliminate the foods you use to distract or medicate yourself—candy, sugary foods, sodas, that extra coffee in the afternoon, carb-laden meals, and unhealthy snacks between meals. Stop eating until you are full and instead eat portions that satisfy.

Tell friends you would like to meet in your home or theirs for dinner, instead of eating out. If you do eat out, choose healthier options on the menu regardless of what the group you are with orders. Items ordered from the pressure of unspoken social cues are generally not as good for you. This is not a book on nutrition, but I encourage you to get your nutrition right. Your body is a system. Your habits feed a lifestyle—spirit, mind, and body. How you treat your body will impact your mind and spirit. And if you are feeding your body junk, this might be an indicator of how you are feeding your mind and spirit, as well.

Gluttony is not a sermon topic we often hear preached from the pulpit. It is just not something about which we like to talk to our American congregations. However, if you clog your body (and your arteries) with bad foods, not only are you endangering your health, but you are also clogging up your spiritual ears. I would guess that, even at wedding feasts, Jesus never ate like the average American at Applebee's.

Steward your physical body. While Paul said that "bodily discipline is only of little profit,"[8] he also said that he "disciplines (his) body and make(s) it (his) slave, so that, after (he has) preached to others, (he himself) will not be disqualified."[9] Combining proper nutrition with some physical exercise can heal as well as any healing prayer service. Taking up walking, running, biking, swimming, weightlifting, or a sport is a healthy way to improve your physical endurance and mental focus. I am not trying to fat-shame anyone, but have you known pastors who have good cause to avoid sermons on slothfulness? If you are one of those, trust me—you are a living sermon to all those in your congregation.

WHAT YOU PUT IN YOUR BODY AND HOW YOU KEEP IT MOVING CAN REOPEN DORMANT SPIRITUAL SENSES THAT YOU HAVE EITHER LONG LOST OR NOT RECENTLY FELT.

It is possible to cut your ministry short by engaging in a sedentary lifestyle or eating habits that invite heart disease, diabetes, physical exhaustion, or—as we have seen in the COVID era—succumbing to an unexpected virus. Discipline your body so that you will not be disqualified from the race. You don't need to run out and join Cross-Fit, though it has its health benefits, but you do need to start somewhere. Jokes about vegans, Jehovah's Witnesses, and Cross-Fit fanatics aside, your health is important to God. What you put in your body and how you keep it moving can reopen dormant spiritual senses that you have either long lost or not recently felt. Hear what God tells you about your health and obey.

Your mental health is also important. Maybe you need to see a counselor. No, I'm not talking about psychotherapy. Perhaps you only need someone to talk to who can help you bring order back into your life. Christian counseling or coaching are both a good start. They are not the only avenues for good mental health, however. Take stock of what you put into your mind daily. Is it stressful? Does it create anxiety? Does it poison your spirit? While drinking to excess can dissipate the Spirit's influence within you, so too can pornography, horror movies, too many video games, the 24-hour news cycle, disturbed sleep cycles, and a host of other mind-wearying activities.

Perhaps you counsel too many people. Reduce your counseling load. Turn off the tv and put down your phone. Be present with others. Learn to listen for understanding. Read a good book. May I suggest picking up your Bible again? Read it for pleasure instead of for research to prepare a message. Engage His Word again, as if for the first time. Soak in worship music for a little while each day. Most of all, slow down. Find things you enjoy doing—a hobby, for instance—and apply yourself to it. Give yourself a break from the work of ministry so that you can be human for a while. You should never draw your identity from your ministry. Find your identity first as His child.

BALANCE YOUR MINISTRY IDENTITY

We tend to identify with our ministries so closely that we often forget we are first and foremost God's children. Ministers try to function with the switch in the "ON" position 24/7. This creates a dual identity. You are one person at home and another when you are at church, defying the definition of integrity. Being "one person"—the same in every situation—is healthier than putting on one mask in one setting and then removing it in another. Your children need to see you acting with integrity, being as gentle at home as you are at church. This might be scary. What if your congregation sees the real you? If they aren't seeing that now, you are doing them a disservice. It would be better for you to leave the church and be true to who you are than to give them a false image to worship and a false hope that they can ever attain to your level of (the appearance of) righteousness.

With that said, work to be an example of righteousness in how you live with integrity. This doesn't mean pretend. If you have flaws but still always move forward in the faith, that alone can inspire people who are deeply flawed and despair that they can never be a truly good Christian— like you. Yes, you want to curb your language in church. You want to live in private what you teach those you lead. However, if you cannot do that at home, at church, in the workplace, and out in public, you have created a house of cards that will eventually come crashing down.

Most ministers panic at the thought that they might be "found out." If your people reject you when they see the real you, they aren't your people. There is so much pressure on ministers to be perfect. Stand against that tide. Be you. Be you constantly being a better you.

There is a reason God chose even the best of men and women in Scripture to offer as examples:

- of hypocrisy (Peter with the Pharisees),

- of unreasonable expectations (Paul with Mark),

- of murderers and adulterers (David and Bathsheba with Uriah),

- of cowards (pick a disciple),

- of braggarts (the Sons of Thunder),

- and a myriad of other flawed characters.

WEARING MASKS TO HIDE WHO YOU ARE IS A LIE THAT WILL ERODE YOUR MENTAL HEALTH.

Jesus alone was perfect. His Spirit is forming His image in you. You're not there yet, and that's okay. Wearing masks to hide who you are is a lie that will erode your mental health.

As one bringing Good News to the unsaved, or as one discipling the saved, you must know who you are in Christ. While that comes with high expectations, gaining the approval of men is not one of them. If you need constant affirmation of your identity, get it from God, not your congregation. We need affirmation from others at times. But what if that all crashes to a halt one day because controversy arises in the church? Who will you be, then?

Will you be the one who seeks peace at all costs, who gives in to the applause of men?

Or will you be the one who is in God's presence daily, who knows His Father's approval?

If you gain your identity from people, your mood will rise with each amen but fall with each criticism.

God alone watches over your identity. His discipline and His praise both exude love.

When you know who you are before Him, no one can shake your spirit. When your identity has been forged in the fires of worship and prayer, you will topple Pharisees and Sadducees. You will be able to stand before governors and kings. You will see Christ seated at the right hand of the Father when the people are coming at you with torches and pitchforks.

Finally, I encourage you to abandon all possessions. No, not your house, clothing, car, and favorite watch. Abandon the idea that the church is yours, the people are yours, or the ministry is yours. Abandon all titles, crowns, and awards. Throw them all at the feet of Jesus. We will all get to Heaven with empty hands. We should learn to live with them empty now. The Church is Christ's Bride, not your possession. You are a steward. The lost belong to Him, too. You are not their savior. This is why it is even more important that you become a healthy messenger.

Padding your achievements to impress people is unseemly and manipulative. Worrying about your church's size when you go to district meetings is a self-destructive comparison game that you cannot win. The pastor with fifty will envy the one with two hundred, and the one with two thousand will envy the one with ten thousand. Steward the people God has given you, remembering that you are His servant and He owns the vineyard. Would it change how you care for them, knowing that they are not yours but His? What ambitions do you deserve to entertain when you realize that it all belongs to Him? He who began a good work in you will complete it. He also will complete it in them. Be guided by His Spirit, and you won't need to lead with your title. When the torches come out, no one cares about your title anyway.

BUILD HEALTHY DECLARATIONS

Declarations from Scripture are powerful ways to change your mindset when you are trapped in negative thought patterns that develop during the process of burnout. They are neither psychobabble nor prosperity-centered incantations. There is nothing unscriptural about resetting our minds according to God's Word. In fact, using declarations is a simple method to practice repentance. We adopt God's thoughts over our own. The thoughts you are correcting in this way are those you may have about God, others, or yourself. Declarations are about acknowledging God's grace, giving it to others, and accepting it for yourself. Declarations correct the perfectionist attitudes and victim mentalities that cause us to spiral into cynicism, doubt, and fear.

Let me give an example of what I have taught in my church and chapel for years. We have a terrible saying that we often toss about when we move in false humility: "I'm just a sinner saved by grace." It carries the truth that we are saved by grace, salted with the lie that we are just sinners. Nothing in the New Covenant says that you are a sinner. In fact, if you have adopted the New Covenant, then you have received forgiveness from your sins and acknowledged the Lordship of Jesus Christ, raised from the dead. You are no longer a sinner but the righteousness of God in Christ. Saying you are a sinner projects a lie about your stature in Christ and is a feeble attempt to absolve yourself of the responsibility to live worthy of your high calling in Him.

Scripture repeatedly calls you a saint, not a sinner. Acknowledging this is not prideful or arrogant. It is simply agreeing with your new nature, a nature purchased for you at the cost of Jesus' blood. You *were* a sinner before your life was radically intersected by the One who sacrificed Himself for you. Yes, it was by His grace; but by it, Christ imputed righteousness to you. If you are still a sinner, you need salvation! Once saved, you will still sin, but your nature is that of the new creation. The old nature is gone, and the new has come. Can you see the string of scriptural affirmations in these paragraphs? Let's look at some more:

About God:

1. God is good. *Psalm 119:68, 143:10, 145:9; Matthew 19:17; Mark 10:18; Luke 18:19*

2. God's kindness, not His wrath, brought me to repentance. *Romans 2:4*

3. Everything He created is good. *1 Timothy 4:4*

4. He gives good and perfect gifts. *Matthew 7:11; Luke 11:13; James 1:17*

5. He has begun a good work in me and will complete it according to His faithfulness. *Philippians 1:6*

6. He works all things together for good for me. *Romans 8:28*

7. His discipline is good, preparing me to share His righteousness. *Hebrews 12:10*

8. He has prepared good things to come. *Hebrews 9:11*

9. He is able to do far more than anything I ask or imagine. His power is at work in me. *Ephesians 3:20*

10. When I confess my sins, He is faithful and just to forgive them and cleanse me from all unrighteousness. *1 John 1:9*

About you (and your brothers and sisters in Christ):

1. God did not give me a spirit of fear, but of power, love, and a sound mind. *2 Timothy 1:7*

2. I am a new creation. *2 Corinthians 5:17*

3. I have been delivered from the power of darkness. *Colossians 1:12-13*

4. Greater is He who is in me than he who is in the world. *1 John 4:4*

5. The Spirit of God dwells in me. *1 Corinthians 3:16*

6. I walk by faith and not by sight. *2 Corinthians 5:7*

7. No weapon formed against me shall prosper. *Isaiah 54:17*

8. I am His child. *1 John 3:1-2*

9. Nothing can separate me from the love of Christ. *Romans 8:35-39*

10. If God is for me, who can be against me? *Romans 8:31*

11. God will complete the good work He started in me. *Philippians 1:6*

12. All things work together for my good. I love God and am called according to His purposes. *Romans 8:28*

13. I am more than a conqueror through Him. He loves me. *Romans 8:37*

14. He can—and will—keep me from falling. *Jude 24*

15. I am the righteousness of God in Christ Jesus. *2 Corinthians 5:20-21*

There are so many more that you can find woven throughout Scripture. In times of darkness, it is important that we remind ourselves who God is to counter the lies of the enemy. If Satan can plant doubt in our faith toward God's goodness and His purpose for our lives, he can undercut our ministry. We also need to remind ourselves that what appears to be happening to us does not change what God says about us or about our future.

WHAT APPEARS TO BE HAPPENING TO US DOES NOT CHANGE WHAT GOD SAYS ABOUT US OR ABOUT OUR FUTURE.

Truth is greater than truth (Truth > truth). A momentary truth (let's say, your disappointment) does not redefine His goodness or your destiny in glory in Him. Your sin in a moment does not change your nature in righteousness. Failure in a season cannot take away your overwhelming victory in eternity. Your changing feelings do not change God, for He does not change and cannot lie. "Let God be found true, though every man *be found* a liar!"[10]

Leaning on such truths and declaring them daily is an antidote to the enemy's poisons. Speaking truth over your feelings and circumstances removes power from his lies. If burnout is anything, it is a long series of lies you have adopted. Once adopted, you subconsciously begin to act on them, empowering the liar. Once acted upon, they produce doubt, fear, and uncertainty. Those feelings are emotionally exhausting, as they are expressions of faith in the devil. Once you accept the lies about yourself, you naturally impose them on others, leading to depersonalization. As your ministry becomes toil, laden with self-doubt and unbelief, you cannot see it being impactful, diminishing your sense of personal accomplishment. This, of course, is the definition of burnout.

REFLECTION

If you are anywhere in the cycle of burnout, I remind you that it need not be permanent. You can leave the ministry treadmill and find the pastureland again.

- Pull away and repent to God. As you make time to be alone, receive His forgiveness, soak in His presence, worship Him, and simply enjoy meditating on His Word. Stay in His presence until you hear His voice again. That is the place to start.

- As your soul finds repose and strength, you can begin to address the habits we discussed that helped bring you low. Do this with God's guidance, covered in grace but resolute in your conviction to change your mindset.

- Try building some declarations of truth within your own devotional time. Remember the *already—not yet* paradox (found in chapter 4). What God says is already true of you but not yet fulfilled. It is biblical, not arrogant, to humbly speak His truths over your situation. If He said it, who are we to argue?

- Below are some declarations I use in my devotional life from Philippians 1, given by verse. I hope you find them helpful:

    1: I am a saint.

    2: God (and Jesus) provides me grace and peace.

    3-4: Others are praying for me.

    5: I am a participant in the Gospel.

    6: God started a *good* work in me. He will perfect it. The day of Christ Jesus is coming.

    9: I am abounding in love in real knowledge and discernment.

    10: I am able to approve what is excellent. I will be sincere and blameless.

    11: I am being filled with the fruit of righteousness which comes through Jesus. This brings glory and praise to God.

    15-16: I preach Christ from good will out of love.

    19: My worst circumstances shall turn out for my deliverance.

    20: I shall not be put to shame in anything. Christ will boldly be exalted in my body, whether by life or by death.

    21: For me, to live is Christ, and to die is gain.

    22: Life in Christ will mean fruitful labor for me.

    27: I conduct myself in a manner worthy of the Gospel of Christ. I strive for the faith of the Gospel together with the saints in one spirit, with one mind.

28: I am not alarmed by those who stand against me. This is a sign of God's salvation in me.

29: It has been granted to me not only to believe in Christ, but also to suffer for His sake. (This is not a bad thing. It is a gift.)

PRAYER OF ENCOURAGEMENT

Father, I have been separated from You too long in a desert wilderness. I admit that I am weary and dry. I long to sense Your presence again. My soul hungers and thirsts after Thee. I repent of believing lies about who I am and who You are. Forgive me. As I fill my mind with Your Word and declare Your Truth over my life, let it sink deeply into my spirit and remind me of who I am in You. Still my heart, and let me not be in a hurry. Have Your way in me, O Lord.

Lead me back to a place where I may hear and know Your voice anew. Show me the good things You have placed in my life and let me see them with new eyes. Put a new song within me, a song of praise to You, that the words of my mouth and the meditation of my heart be again acceptable in Thy sight. Give me a heart of flesh and wash my mind with the water of the Word until all my service to You flows from fathomless gratitude—grateful praise because You bought me with a price and made me Your own. I acknowledge that I am a new creation. I am made righteous in You, and therefore I have hope. In Christ Jesus, amen.

ENDNOTES

1   John 10:9.

2   Foss, Richard Wayne. "Burnout among Clergy and Helping Professionals: Situational and Personality Correlates." (Ph.D. diss., Fuller Theological Seminary, 2002), 16.

3   See 2 Samuel 6 and 1 Chronicles 13.

4   See Proverbs 4:23

5   C.S. Lewis, *The Problem of Pain*, London 1942.

6   Tell All My Friends (Album). "Not In A Hurry" (Official Video) © 2017 by Will Reagan & United Pursuit. You can find this song at https://www.youtube.com/watch?v=VeWuavHf4oY.

7   Joel 2:25.

8   1 Timothy 4:8.

9   1 Corinthians 9:27.

10   Romans 3:4.

CHAPTER SEVEN

COMMUNITY IN THE PASTURELANDS

*"But the one who enters by the door
is a shepherd of the sheep."[1]*

*"Feeling socially isolated activates neurobiological
mechanisms that may promote self-preservation in the
short-term but take a toll on health and well-being in
the long-term... Among these effects are higher vascular
resistance in young adults, the putative consequence
of the brain's hypervigilance for social threats; larger
morning rises in cortisol, a powerful stress hormone,
the consequence of the brain's preparation for another
dangerous day; increased prepotent responding, which
means that behaviors high in the response hierarchy are
more likely even though this includes impulsive (including
poor health) behaviors; altered gene expression, for instance,
increasing inflammatory biology to deal with assaults; and
the decreased salubriousness of sleep, the consequence
of the brain's high alert state. Together, these processes
can contribute to early morbidity and mortality."[2]*

WE ARE NOT THERE YET

Normally, it would be considerate to ask you to put down this book and continue seeking God while putting chapter six into practice for a while. However, you are very much like an addict at this point. You cannot trust yourself to make wise decisions about your health and ministry quite yet. You also should not trust that you might pick up the book again while there are additional things you must do to get healthy.

Like an addict after detox, you may have the tendency to awaken to the bright, sunshiny morning, feeling alive again and ready to tackle the world. That was quick! Now you can get back to running that church, or taking unlimited 911 calls, or counseling with a new sense of mission. You have a rush of adrenaline and endorphins, aided by a venti quad-shot coffee with six sugars, making you feel like it is all behind you. The burnout has faded into the past. There is clearly no need for more self-care or further groveling before God. He has stamped your release papers, and you can go at it again now that you have more energy and a renewed sense of purpose.

I once responded to a call as a young police officer to deliver the bad news to a woman that her brother had overdosed on heroin. He had been a drug user for years and had just served a three-year prison sentence. When he got out, it didn't even take a day for him to get back to the habit. However, when he took the same dose that he had used before prison—where he had been clean for three years—it was far more than his body could handle. His first injection became his last.

We feel better when we first cast off the chains of months or years of striving. We enhance that feeling with returning to the healthy spiritual, physical, and mental practices that gave us life before we crashed. I caution you that this is only a honeymoon period. It may feel great, but you are not ready to take on a full load of ministry after a brief period of detox. The drive within has returned. The pressure from outside has not changed. But your internal capacity is still fragile, and the wounds are still healing. Like the addict who died on his first dose after three years clean, you can quickly destroy the progress you have been making if you dive back into the same dosage of ministry you used to mainline.

Most who recognize burnout and seek to adjust do not scale back ministry efforts. Instead, they **add** God on the side. Maybe they start running again a few days a week, and perhaps they tweak their diet just a bit. They play with the idea of fixing their burnout but are not truly committed to it.

Does that strike close to home?

If that description fits you, I strongly suggest going back two chapters and persisting in your journey toward health.

You may even have skipped the book's introduction, rationalizing that your burnout isn't that bad or that you are a quick study. "Just show me what to do, and I've got it!" Taking a shortcut is trying to access the pastureland by entering another way.

Jesus points out that those who do so are thieves and robbers, and His sheep won't listen to them.[3] You cannot bring life to others that way; you will only bring death, loss, and destruction. Hurt people hurt people …

… but hurt ministers can destroy them.

HURT PEOPLE HURT PEOPLE …

… BUT HURT MINISTERS CAN DESTROY THEM

GETTING YOUR LEGS BACK

It was immediately evident that I had ruptured my Achilles tendon. I returned from Iraq and wanted our family to join an activity we could enjoy together. In the cold, rainy Northwest winters, choosing a martial art is one option for staying healthy and working out together, so we embarked on a journey into taekwondo. Six months in, I felt amazing. I am certain my estimation of my abilities was much higher than anyone watching me, but I was enjoying another day of sparring ... until I was lying flat on my back, my left Achilles throbbing with pain. They said I screamed like a little girl, but I am most certain they were exaggerating. Besides, that was a rude comment to make about little girls.

The hospital nurses were just as kind as my sparring partners. They seemed to have me pegged:

Nurse: "Are you forty?"

Me: "In a few weeks; why?"

Nurse: "Basketball?"

Me: "No."

Her: "Softball?"

Me: "No."

Her: "Martial arts?"

Me: ....

Bingo. It seems that we humans share many things in common—such as forty-ish men starting some foolish physical fitness activity and going at it as if they were still in their twenties. The same phenomenon happens in ministry burnout. When we reach burnout, we all want to get back on the horse quickly and resume our former pace.

I know a minister who was in over his head. He didn't have the education, depth of Spirit, or accountability he needed to take on a large church. He ran headlong into the offer anyhow, thinking he could always catch up—and besides, who needs accountability?

It caught up to him years later when he had to step down from his pulpit after being accused of unfaithfulness in his marriage. It is a common theme, just like the man Pastor Jim brought on staff, who was still hurting from a previous disappointment but pressed into more and more ministry before his family was healed.

Pace is important.

So is healing from former wounds.

We need certain things to help us sustain a successful ministry of any size or type. The most important of these is fellowship. Accordingly, Jesus has allowed others through the Door into the pasture. They are there for your benefit, and you for theirs. Before you go wildly trying to run in and out of the pasture, make sure you are first using the Door instead of jumping the fence.

- Is God telling you to re-engage with ministry?
- At what level?
- And what ministry, specifically?

This may be where He is telling you to "Go to a land that I will show you."[4] When I closed my ministries and ran, I was pretty sure I heard Him command that. So, I obeyed. Maybe God is telling you to dip your toe back into the same ministry you backed out of to alleviate your burnout symptoms. But perhaps He is saying, "Just the toe, for now."

You must unconditionally surrender in order to give God the space He has ordained to knit your fractured life back into one, integrated whole. Having integrity does not just mean being honest. It means being the same person in every circumstance. After recognizing the onset of burnout, you must learn to walk in integrity again.

IF YOU ARE IN ADVANCED BURNOUT, YOUR FAMILY HAS BEEN SEEING AND FEELING IT, TOO.

Here is a bitter pill to swallow: If you are in advanced burnout, your family has been seeing and feeling it, too.

If you won't slow down for yourself, perhaps you will consider the impact of your burnout on them. A person with integrity will not allow their family to suffer. That healing must come for everyone—after all, your first ministry is to them. They must also learn what it is to find freedom in the pasturelands.

SPOUSES

I hope your spouse has been your biggest supporter in your ministry. They have watched you burn the candle at both ends. They have felt your pain, endured your wild mood swings (some of which turned against them), and may well have been trying to warn you for years. My wife had been cautioning me, but I tried to plow on through the trials, unwittingly creating more difficulties for myself that were entirely unnecessary.

Our once vibrant prayer life had fallen off to occasional prayer together, mostly over meals and when an urgent need arose. We used to enjoy a book together weekly, but had altogether stopped reading new books, much less the Bible. We were (and are) still in love today. She had endured much for church and chaplaincy, but now we both needed healing.

We are still in that process.

Part of our healing journey is to allow ourselves space to hear God again. We know we have more ministry in our future, but we need time, and we both recognize it. We have talked about it. I must admit that I probably have not been as open with her about my struggles—a realization that comes even as I write this book. I am a writer, and this is my therapy. I now send her each new chapter to read so that I can better communicate my thoughts and feelings.

There. I said it.

F-e-e-l-i-n-g-s.

You guys may know what I mean. Like colors, men claim to have a limited palette of feelings. We see red, yellow, green, blue, orange, purple, black, and white. We are happy, angry, full, hungry, and horny. Our wives want us to pick the new paint shade, "Do you like the eggshell, cream, alabaster, gardenia, or sand dollar?"

"Um, sure. Whatever you like, dear," we answer.

In the same way, they also want to know how we feel. Many of us would rather make the effort to pick the right shade of white. Just so you know, out of the emotions I listed above, "happy" is the only real emotion among them. I hate to admit it, but we must learn to expand our feelings palette. Our wives need to know how we are feeling. They need this to understand how they can help.

Here is a test to give your spouse if you dare. Ask, "On a scale of one to ten, how would you rate our marriage?" Your spouse will usually have a different answer than you do. After our first year of marriage, I was surprised to find that a marriage that I rated a nine received a mere six from my wife. It improved to a seven within a year but remained between seven and eight for the longest time. I have recently been able to nudge it up to a nine, but I have always been a point or so higher on my satisfaction scale regarding our marriage. The follow-up question is even more daring: "How can I help grow our marriage by one more point?"

I offer this tool because, if you are married, your spouse is your most important ministry partner. Ministry should not be something you do independently from your spouse. That is what we call "work." Whether or not they are *in* ministry, your call makes them ministers in their own right. They minister to you and your children. Your people will likely look to them for guidance and as an example, and they need to know how to help you decompress from your church, chaplaincy, coffee shop, or evangelism efforts. No one sees you like your spouse. They can tell you when you are losing your integrity. They need to see you ministering out of who you are at home, not just by what you have achieved on paper or what your community says of you. Your spouse can be your greatest source of healing from sheep bites—*if* you let them into your thoughts *and feelings* and listen to their input.

IF YOU ARE MARRIED, MINISTRY SHOULD NOT BE SOMETHING YOU DO INDEPENDENTLY FROM YOUR SPOUSE.

FELLOW MINISTERS

This can be intimidating. I left the fellowship of a denomination because it had become so focused on church growth that the denominational pastors in my area had become quite guarded. They did not seem to want to befriend other pastors in the area. I presume this was because of shortcomings they felt about not raking in the numbers in the pews since that was the focus of the district leadership. There were no rewards at district meetings for faithfulness in ministry unless it was accompanied by something tangible like a new church building project to house all the new people you were attracting. Perhaps you have experienced this, too?

Chaplains often have a natural affinity for other chaplains. There is no pressure to have the coolest worship band or compare attendance numbers. Chaplains tend to gather around relational compassion. They know that other chaplains have gone through the same stuff they are going through, and this makes them trustworthy confidants. In fact, many chaplains do not share much of what they see in their ministry with their pastors, family, or fellow (civilian) Christians because they know most of them do not understand the gore and trauma to which chaplains are exposed.

One chaplain offered this incisive commentary:

> *Just discussing what a hanging actually looks like ... I mean, the vast majority of people can't comprehend that. I would be hurting them by asking them to participate in my remembrance of it. I don't know that the average pastoral staff is necessarily well equipped to support first responder chaplains.*

A chaplain who has just conducted combat ministry for a dying soldier and his unit or responded to the scene of a multiple homicide and had to walk his officers through the aftermath knows another chaplain will listen and understand. They will be there when they are needed. More importantly, when a firefighter dies on the operating table, and the firehouse needs their constant presence, the fire chaplain knows that another first responder chaplain has felt that pain and will understand the post-traumatic stress that inevitably follows.

They will comfort without judgment. They know to check up on you in the days that follow.

I do not mean to beat up on pastors here. One of the best groups I have ever had the privilege of finding fellowship with was a group of four other pastors in my city who were not in my denomination. We represented five different denominations or independent churches, and we shared with one another from the heart. We prayed for each other's families and congregants. Pastors need the fellowship of other pastors, just as chaplains need the fellowship of other chaplains. Most of all, they need friendships within their sectors of ministry. Pastoral isolation is one of the largest stressors that create the conditions for burnout in ministry. Pastoring is lonely enough as an occupation. It is even lonelier when you are pastoring alone.

ISOLATION IS ONE OF THE LARGEST STRESSORS THAT CREATE THE CONDITIONS FOR BURNOUT IN MINISTRY.

In many ways, as a pastor, I wish other pastors had the kind of kinship with fellow clergy that military, hospital, and first responder chaplains find naturally. I don't know how the Church has become so demanding of pastors that it has driven many into isolation. Pastors need vital relationships with other pastors, especially within their cities or areas of ministry. The walls of hostility were destroyed in Jesus Christ, yet we still seem to erect new walls according to peripheral doctrines, vainly imagined territories, cautious denominations, and comparative church sizes. For you pastors who have felt the same as I have in these matters, I pray over you with Jesus that we may all be one. May we all have a strong enough identity to cherish our traditions while uniting our efforts to fulfill the Great Commission.

MENTORS AND CONFIDANTS

There are people in your churches that want to see you as a normal human being before they accept you as their pastor. Chaplains also need to be seen as real-life humans by their Soldiers, Sailors, Marines, Airmen, (Spacemen? Sorry, Space Force—I'm not yet sure how to cover you), Coast Guardsmen, police officers, firefighters, EMTs, doctors, nurses, and patients. Let me share a secret: You may feel the need to be all-godly, but you are also all-human. Yes, you are the example to whom many look for faith. Denying your humanity is how that fracture in your integrity started. You need people around you, close to you, who are not in the ministry. They will never approach you unless you, as a fellow human, show yourself approachable.

One of the things that kept me healthy as a cop was fellowshipping with people who were not cops. The quickest way cops spiral into dysfunction in their lives is by surrounding themselves in their social circles exclusively with other cops. I knew an officer who had an amazing marriage to an amazing woman who was also a cop. He started hanging around with other cops, several of whom were divorced. Before long, he had adopted their cynical attitude about marriage. Their venomous language about their exes poisoned his relationship with his wife. Their good marriage ended up in a bad divorce.

We need healthy relationships outside of our professional circles. It keeps us in touch with reality. Few can survive the myopic view of life one acquires from a limited, incestuous circle of friends. When all you see around you are other ministers on treadmills, you will eventually jump on a treadmill, yourself. Confirmation bias cripples the renewing of the mind.

CONFIRMATION BIAS CRIPPLES THE RENEWING OF THE MIND.

I was blessed to have many friends within my church. We shared openly about our lives with one another, even if we didn't share much in common outside of church. Like Jesus, I held a few in my church and chaplaincy as close friends. They would check on me regularly to see how I was doing, and I felt comfortable sharing my struggles with them (most of the time). I still stay in touch with many of them. I had a few friends among my officers, one of whom met with me regularly for coffee. The comfort and counsel were not merely one-way.

One frustration in my life has always been finding a mentor—or what might be called a father in the faith. From my earliest years, I longed for that one person I could say, decades later, had been a father to me. While I have many who fit the role for a time, I never had a consistent, close mentor or father in the faith. I have not yet cracked that code, so if you can find a spiritual father or mother, cherish them. Lean into them. Tell them what they mean to you. Knowing there is someone you can go to with your innermost sorrows, someone who can speak life into your soul, someone who can counsel you through trials, is a blessing that many long for and few truly find. I have had good mentors, fathers from afar, and a few with whom I could share deeply. However, I feel I have missed out on one of God's best gifts in a man I could call my spiritual father.

LIFE-GIVING PRACTICES

You need a hobby. You need vacations—real ones that don't require a vacation from which to recover. You need a motorcycle. You need season tickets to your favorite sport, although football tends to be a problem on Sundays for pastors. You need a ministry apart from your ministry—somewhere you can act in your gifting away from the people who have heard all your sermon illustrations and stories, or for whom you have already prayed innumerable times for healing.

My wife and I have had just two, two-week vacations throughout our marriage. Both came as a result of deployments; one after Iraq and one when I came home from Afghanistan for emergency leave to conduct my grandmother's funeral. However, we did one thing I would never change. We went on mission trips to China with our kids as a group from our church. They were hardship trips, to be sure, taking us to places with dirty hotels, headache-inducing altitudes, and food we had to eat without looking too carefully. We didn't understand the language, though our hosts translated for us. However, we engaged in wonderful ministry to amazing people groups. We got out of our cultural isolation and experienced the extraordinary bond of the Spirit with other Christians, many of whom were suffering for their faith in ways we had never experienced.

I have also been to Tanzania to minister to Christian school staff, share at a conference, preach at a crusade, and teach local pastors at a friend's school. While I always came home exhausted, it was the kind of exhaustion that causes you to sleep deeply and awake refreshed (*salubrious* sleep). I found myself happy to give up the trivial theme park experiences to pour out what God has placed in me to others. Every time I go to the mission field, I come back with more than I brought. I learn more from the people I minister to than I perhaps impart to them. It has been food for my soul, and I consider it my hobby and my choice of vacation.

You need to learn to read the Bible again for the first time. You have your study times, but what about reading it for the joy of hearing Him speak through it, as if just to you? If the Word does not speak to you, how can you possibly speak of it to others? As His minister to the Church—inside or outside the four walls—you must learn to hear His voice narrating His story to you. Only then can you offer it with joy to others.

You should read books by Christian authors and watch shows by Christian writers that inspire you. They are not God's Word in the same way that the Bible is, but they are written by creative people who are gifted to experience God in a way that may be new to you. Read the Church Fathers. Read *Pilgrim's Progress*. Read Francis Chan. Read C.S. Lewis. By all means, read Lewis! Read Francis Schaefer. Read *God's Generals*. Read Watchman Nee. Read devotionals and read theology. Only, do it for pleasure, not research. Don't do it just for the quotes you can get for your next sermon.

Go camping. Spend time in nature. Explore the country. Get outside and talk to God in the wilderness. That seems to have some biblical precedent. Go horseback riding. Learn to surf. I sold my house, got rid of most of my possessions, and bought an RV!

Take bachata dance lessons with your spouse—or whatever the two of you find exciting. Do whatever it is that reminds you of the joy you entered into the ministry with in the first place. If you have no life in you, what good are you at the pulpit, in the station house, or on the cancer ward? I know these are not *ministry* things, but you may find ministry opportunities—or you may be ministered to—along the way.

You will pour out to others only what you have in your cup.

Here is something that may be well outside of your comfort zone: try a treasure hunt. Prayerfully ask God to show you a) where to go, b) a description of a person you may meet there, and c) a need they have for which you can pray. Listen for His voice. Risk trusting it. Then go and be surprised that God spoke to you and equipped you to bless that very person He showed you in your sanctified imagination. This may take some practice, but it is well worth it when you see what God will do when you trust Him. It's not *church* ministry, but I have found it to be an incredible way to get outside of my box and experience ministry the way Jesus did it. There's a sermon in there, somewhere …

All your outings are opportunities for ministry. When you go to a store, don't go just to get what you need. Go expecting to run into someone who needs healing prayer, who wants to offload their cares, or who needs Jesus right now. Ask the woman at the check stand or the barista at the coffee shop if you can pray for them, and then pray for them aloud, right there. I used to go to the same, rather unkempt gas station regularly because of three clerks there who needed ministry. One cried every time I prayed for her, one felt relief from fibromyalgia when I prayed for her, and I made some good progress with a guy who liked to debate atheism versus Christianity.

If that is not your style, try volunteering at a homeless shelter, food bank, crisis pregnancy center, or hospital. Don't do it as a church program; do it because God wants you to reach the downtrodden, the widow, and the orphan. Expand your idea of ministry beyond the church walls. God cannot be locked inside a box, but that box will easily imprison you.

EXPAND YOUR IDEA OF MINISTRY BEYOND THE CHURCH WALLS— GOD CANNOT BE LOCKED INSIDE A BOX, BUT THAT BOX WILL EASILY IMPRISON YOU.

Returning to the ministry where you burned out is not your only option. You don't need to leave it, but you do need perspective. You need fresh fire. Oftentimes, we feel that the Spirit is stagnant in the ministry environment with which we have become so familiar. We have prayed for that woman's marriage a hundred times. We have sought healing for that man's cancer for years. We have preached the same message, and no one has budged. We don't even notice the broken water fountain, the stained ceiling tiles, the dying sound system, or the monotonality of the same old greetings at church anymore. We sing the same songs, observe the same liturgy, and follow the same rituals.

Familiarity breeds contempt.

Get uncomfortable for a while.

Jesus did not say, "Stay, therefore, and continue with the same old same old." He said, "Go!"

Let the Spirit breathe life back into your faith. Act like you are not a pastor, chaplain, or denominational leader. Pretend for a while that you are a follower of Jesus Christ. Cleanse lepers. Heal the sick. Raise the dead. Cast out demons. Shout the Gospel from your rooftop. Find a worthy person in another city and dine with them. Go door to door offering prayer. Take your family on a mission vacation. Introduce yourself to your next-door neighbors. Make every service for a month into prayer and worship time—no message, no crazy schedule, no frills. Just your people and you seeking God's presence.

Do something different and shake up your routine.

You may find that God moves in ways you never anticipated. You may find He still wants to use *you* in ways you never imagined. There are more than one thousand ways to get your legs back, and none of them have to be in the ministry that burned you out. Go in and out. Find the pastureland. Just make sure you enter through the Door.

Pretty soon, you will find yourself running again. This time, it will be toward something, and it won't feel like the drudgery of a treadmill.

REFLECTION

We need people in our lives who can speak life over us, provide guidance, give perspective, support us, and remind us of who we are in times both good and bad. We especially need those from whom we can learn new lessons, receive fresh fire, hear prophetic counsel, and regain a vision of a hopeful future.

> *"As for the things you have learned and received*
> *and heard and seen in Me, practice these things;*
> *and the God of peace shall be with you."*
> PHILIPPIANS 4:9

- Make a list of those you have in your life who provide this kind of support.

- Perhaps take a moment to contact one of them to share what you have been reflecting on regarding burnout. If you are married, make that your first conversation.

- Who are your fathers or mothers in the faith? If you have none, pray that God will provide them.

- Make a list of the healthy practices you have previously engaged in, those you are presently doing, and those you may wish to try.

- Reflect on your concept of what your ministry looks like and the pace you keep. Are you willing to lay that down if He leads? What would that look like?

PRAYER OF ENCOURAGEMENT

Father, thank You for those You have given me to encourage my heart, give counsel, and hold me accountable. I honor them and gratefully acknowledge Your hand in our connection. I receive them as Your gift for my life.

I come to You with fresh hope stirring in my soul, yearning to feel joy in Your presence again as I seek You for You—not to check a box, prepare for a message, or fulfill an assignment. Stir curiosity in me. A spirit of adventure. Help me awaken each morning with the wonder of a child and approach the day in awe of Your greatness and excited to see what You want to show me and where You want me to walk with You.

Thank You for being the Door through which I can enter the pastureland. Forgive me for jumping the fence so often. Today I embrace only the possibilities You place before me, and I release the things I have obligated myself to without continuing to listen for Your voice as I endeavor. Here am I, send me. In Christ Jesus, amen.

ENDNOTES
1   John 10:2.

2   Cacioppo, John T. and Stephanie Cacioppo. "Social Relationships and Health: The Toxic Effects of Perceived Social Isolation." *Social and Personality Psychology Compass* 8, no. 2 (2014): 72.

3   John 10:7-9.

4   Genesis 12:1.

CHAPTER EIGHT

PUTTING FIRST THINGS FIRST—YOUR CALLING[1]

"Therefore, I exhort the elders among you, as your fellow elder…, shepherd the flock of God among you, exercising oversight not under compulsion, but voluntarily, according to the will of God; and not for sordid gain, but with eagerness; nor yet as lording it over those allotted to your charge, but proving to be examples to the flock. And when the Chief Shepherd appears, you will receive the unfading crown of glory."[2]

"Research indicates that clergy simultaneously experience burnout and ministry satisfaction. Given the extensive literature on stressors experienced by clergy, we anticipated that clergy may experience above-average rates of burnout. However, this was not the case. It may be that pastoral ministry is an experience of emotional extremes, and the joy or meaningfulness of ministry may be a protective factor against experiencing all three components of burnout."[3]

GETTING YOUR CALLING RIGHT

As a chaplain, I tell all those I train that they cannot be effective chaplains unless they love the people God has given them, saved and unsaved. As a pastor, I have been constantly focused on how best to love the people God has given to me. However, had I sought out a ministry career because it looked like a suitable profession, that it made good money, because I desired to help people, or that it was just a good way to stave off boredom, I could never have loved the people the way a pastor must. To shepherd people, one *must* experience an undeniable sense of *calling* and then decide to express that calling with a conscious act of the will—to love others.

> **TO SHEPHERD PEOPLE, ONE *MUST* EXPERIENCE AN UNDENIABLE SENSE OF *CALLING* AND THEN DECIDE TO EXPRESS THAT CALLING WITH A CONSCIOUS ACT OF THE WILL—TO LOVE OTHERS.**

I focused my study on examining how to better link chaplains with their pastors, endorsers, and denominational representatives to mitigate the impact of burnout. One of the precursors to seeking a relationship with church leaders is the awareness that ministers are called—and that calling is to a pastoral ministry, regardless of the ministerial position in which they wind up. This awareness requires support for their calling.

One chaplain said he hoped that my study would bring about education "for chaplains, as well as for churches, that would encourage them to find means of support because meeting people in crisis situations can be a bit draining." The theological foundation of the study is that the most essential place any minister should find affirmation and support is through a combination of God's call on the minister's life *and* the formal recognition and support of the Church. Think of it in trinitarian terms:

- God is, of course, the Father who chooses the beloved Son;
- the Church is the Spirit that breathes life into ministry, and
- the minister is like Jesus, the incarnate representation of God to the world.

All three should be in unity.

GOD'S CALL

There is little I can tell you that can quantify what God's call feels like. It likely looks quite different for everyone. However, like wondering if that special someone you have been dating is *the one*, hearing God's call is something unique. You must experience it to know it. I know people who have heard His audible voice giving them explicit instructions. I have heard from some that they were not certain until someone prophesied it over them. Most pastors I have asked about it just knew that they knew—it was an inward *knowing* that defies explanation.

Such a calling often manifests in certain gifts within a person. They may have unique insight and understanding of Scripture beyond their peers. They may be excellent writers and speakers. They may be natural leaders. They may have had a deep, inquisitive disposition toward faith and God from as early as they can remember. They may carry a burden for lost souls or a deep desire to connect people with God. Whatever the case, they feel a call.

Awareness of the call is also an experience unique to each minister. Sometimes it hits like lightning through a single, momentous event in their life. Sometimes the person simply and quite naturally starts doing pastoral things, in church or outside of church, and the call just becomes obvious to all. However one comes about their calling, most report that it is often clearer to them in retrospect than in advance.

Whether your calling comes to the pastorate or to another ministry field (such as chaplaincy, evangelism, or missions), you must first recognize the *pastoral* foundation of your call—shepherding God's people. While this is most easily identified among pastors called to local church ministry, chaplains and other non-pulpit ministers are not exempt from pastoring Christians who may well be present in their ministry sector. Whether sent to an unreached people group, assigned to preach in an itinerant ministry evangelizing the lost, or caring for the saved and unsaved within police and fire departments, the military, or hospitals, non-pastoral positions require the pastoral basics. The foundational skill set for any ministry includes the ability to teach, to counsel, to console, to guide, to correct, and to share the love of Christ.

In other words, if God calls you to ministry, He calls you first and foremost to be a shepherd, and in that vocation, to shepherd a people. Therefore, the inward call to ministry one feels is always outwardly directed toward a people group. Which form of ministry you eventually follow will always express itself in a trajectory toward a specific audience.

A felt call to Africa, for instance, must eventually find its way to a country, a town, or an ethnic group within Africa. Even the greatest missionaries have either focused on one tribe or the lost souls of a nation. Few have a continental or global reach. It is wise to remember that you are limited in time and space. If God needed only you to reach the world, He would have raptured everyone else and left you to do the work. If you still feel you are called to reach the universe, I urge you to read chapter five again.

I want to make a special note for my fellow chaplains: You, too, must sense this calling from God and find your people.

When you find your people, you must also follow through with the second part of defining your calling. You need the recognition of your calling by the Body of Christ. Too many chaplains feel the call but also feel burdened by all the red tape that seems to come with getting the training and affirmation of their local church body. Many of the chaplains in my study who were not connected to a local church body exhibited the highest burnout rates.

> **YOU NEED THE RECOGNITION OF YOUR CALLING BY THE BODY OF CHRIST.**

CONFIRMATION

A person must *desire* the pastoral call. "It is a trustworthy statement: if any man aspires to the office of overseer, *it is* a fine work he desires *to do*."[4] But desire is not confirmation. The local church, like any other group, sometimes devolves into a cult of personality. Men and women in any organization seeking power, fame, or validation from others can wrongly aspire to leadership simply because of desire. Wrong desires must be sifted and discerned within the Body of Christ.

There are many personal qualifications for ministry spelled out in 1 Timothy 3 (for both overseers and deacons), Titus 1:5-9, and as above in 1 Peter 5:1-4. I must caveat these requirements, however. If the original disciples had been weighed by these qualifications, it is unlikely that Peter, James, and John, much less Paul, would have been permitted to any church office. In fact, if we are honest with ourselves, how many of us would pass a strict interpretation of each and every qualification?

Spiritual discernment must be applied when gauging the present situation of pastoral candidates *and* the trajectory of their lives along the path toward holiness. In any event, Scripture does provide us with a starting rubric for assessing a candidate's overall capacity for ministry. It gives us desirable personal traits for candidates that are comprehensive but may be so exclusive that they make "perfect" the enemy of "good." It is also true that some who appear perfect may well be padding their resume while others who appear less qualified are on a trajectory for growth that belies their present stature. Only Spirit-led church leadership can rightly discern the calling and qualification of an individual. After all, God sees the heart, not just what we see.

Ultimately, the local body or denominational representative is appointed by God with the charge to ordain leaders within the church. This means that your mere sense of calling must be tested by human red tape. It would take many more chapters for me to exposit the brief theology of calling and appointment that I offered in my thesis, but that is not my goal. It should suffice to say that once you know you are called, you should submit yourself to the process of the body in which you are found when God calls you.

This submission to the body is difficult for many, especially women. A church may permit women to serve in certain ministry capacities but then shy away when they express a call to pastoral ministry. Some churches advertise that up front. They will not ordain women. Period. Full stop.

Other churches will give women ministerial credentials but stop short of allowing them to teach men, especially in the greater congregation. Some churches permit full ordination of women. Once again, my intent here is not to argue for or against a particular theology. However, if God *placed* you in the Catholic church, you must decide whether He *called* you there. If so, you must discover the ministry to which He called you that fits within the constraints of a Catholic theology of women in ministry.

Likewise, some chaplains in my study felt called but found their leadership didn't recognize that calling. In a few cases I examined, it was a simple matter of the leaders not understanding the chaplaincy ministry the person was seeking. The chaplains had shrugged it off, not realizing that their guidance and oversight were integral to their success. The church leadership was familiar with people wanting to become pastors but not with people with a desire to pursue chaplaincy.

Regardless of the possible hurdles or potential complications, seek affirmation for your calling where God called you.

In rare circumstances, God may nudge you to move to a more suitable setting for your desired ministry—one that is uniquely suited to understand and support you in the particular ministry to which you feel called.

In the matter of church affirmation of your call, patience is a virtue. Rushing your calling can be a sign of pride or selfish ambition. If God took forty years to mold Moses for a forty-year ministry, certainly you can wait a few years for Him to establish you in yours. If God required three years of on-the-job training for the disciples, He might rightly ask you to commit to a four-year degree or even a follow-on master's degree. Maybe you'll get lucky, and your leaders will cast lots that fall upon you, as the disciples did to elevate Matthias to Judas' vacant position. Luck is not God's standard method. If you will not go through the process for qualification and recognition of your calling, it is unlikely anyone will respect your desire for a miraculous, easy appointment.

Short of hoping for a Judas to gift you a vacant position, you should be patient with the process your church has assigned everyone who wants to enter formal ministry representing them.

Church and denominational requirements are often built on years of assessing what creates a successful minister. They are also adopted to ensure that unworthy applicants aren't rushed through to a leadership position in which they will likely fail and bring reproach upon Christ and His Church. When you ask a church to affirm your ministry, you ask them to place people in your spiritual care. Ordination or commissioning should never be light or trivial matters. Paul directed Timothy to never be hasty in the laying on of hands.[5] Here we must turn to how calling and affirmation may affect long-term ministerial health.

ORDINATION OR COMMISSIONING SHOULD NEVER BE LIGHT OR TRIVIAL MATTERS.

CHAPLAINS IN THE STUDY

Two telling demographics emerged among the first responder chaplains in the study: the nature of their sending sources and their relationships with their local churches. These are shown in the pie charts following. Those with no sending source or who consider themselves "self-sent" represented 26% of the group, or seven of the twenty-seven participants. This closely approximates the number I found who lacked a sending source during the informal polling in my classes (approximately one-fourth to one-third). In addition, three chaplains indicated they had no relationship with a local church congregation. Two-thirds of the participants stated they were engaged in some level of leadership with their local church community. During interviews, these chaplains stated their positions included senior or associate pastor, deacon, elder, or other ministry leadership.

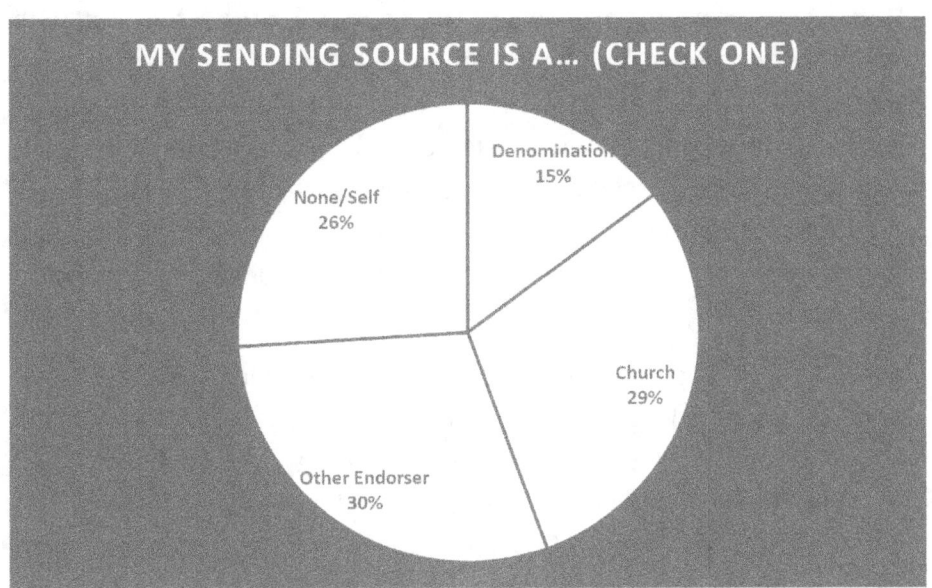

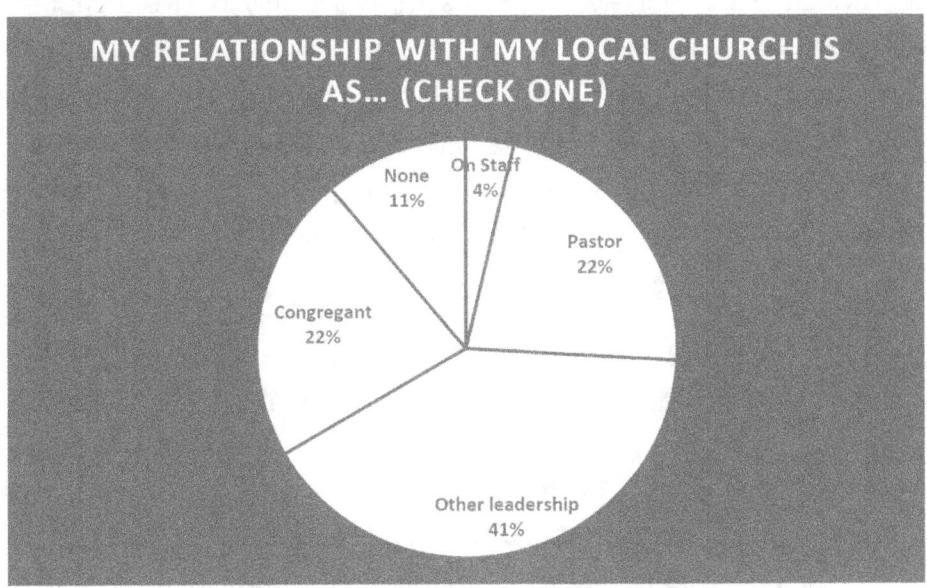

When comparing each chaplain's perception of their burnout with their connection to a sending source, quantitative data failed to show a significant correlation. However, during the qualitative interviews (breakdown following), I found a definite, negative correlation to burnout for chaplains whose relationship with the local church was tenuous or non-existent. Conversely, there was strong evidence that a good relationship with local church leaders provided a degree of insulation from burnout.

Only eight participants said they had no sending source,[6] while seventeen stated a local church was their sending source. One chaplain was sent directly by his denomination, bypassing the local church, and one identified his sending source as an "other endorser." There was some confusion among the chaplains about what a sending source was, despite having the definition provided to them. In the initial survey, seven identified themselves as self-sent, while only twelve identified their churches as senders.

Those who held an ordination or license as a pastor in a church showed less confusion and easily identified their church or denomination as their sending source. Five of the seven "self-sent" participants were pastors who admitted during the First Responder Chaplain (FRC) interviews that their church was their source of ordination and approved of their FRC ministry. Sixteen participants indicated that they had received some form of formal ceremony, prayer, or blessing as a commissioning or ordination into ministry. Almost all of those ceremonies were conducted with prayer and the laying on of hands in front of the congregation or a smaller group of church leadership.

The remaining eleven participants did not receive any ceremony or formal recognition—what I defined as an affirmation—before a congregation or leadership. Five of these chaplains received some minimal form of endorsement from their church. This recognition often came as a letter from the pastor or an associate, addressed to a chaplaincy organizational agency, stating that they approved the candidate for ministry as a first responder chaplain. This type of letter does not imply that the pastor understands what the ministry itself entails, only that they acknowledged that one of their parishioners required a letter of approval.

Here is a quick breakdown, so the numbers are easier to digest:

- **Total participants—27.**
- **Received formal recognition, license, or ceremony—16.**

  These chaplains were ordained, licensed, held a pastoral role in their church, or were formally recognized and sent by the church for chaplaincy ministry.

- **Received <u>no</u> formal recognition, license, or ceremony—11.**

  Of these 11 participants, five had received only a letter of approval to become a chaplain.

- **Indicated they had no sending source—8.**

  Although several had received letters approving their chaplaincy, they did not feel connected to their church as part of their chaplaincy ministry.

- **Reported no connection to a local church or other sending source—3.**

Of the twenty-seven chaplains, most accurately identified their burnout level in advance of taking the first FBI. The following review includes their estimations and a look at the five chaplains who scored highest in self-reported burnout, measured as low Personal Accomplishment (PA) versus Emotional Exhaustion (EE), or EE within two points of PA.

Self-Assessment Results:

- **Accurately evaluated their own burnout—20.**

  Note: when comparing their self-perception versus what their FBI scores indicated.

- **Overestimated their level of burnout—1.**

- **Underestimated their level of burnout—6.**
  Note: 22% of chaplains underestimated their burnout level.

Five Highest Self-Reported Burnout Subjects:
(See the FBI Burnout Scores chart from Chapter 4, following.)

- One chaplain (P16)* accurately self-reported their burnout level as "To a Great Extent." This chaplain had already begun the process of leaving the chaplaincy.

    This chaplain's initial FBI scores:
    Personal Accomplishment (PA)—4.
    Emotional Exhaustion (EE)—9.

- The chaplain (P20) who exhibited the highest burnout indication was admittedly overworked between a day job, chaplaincy, and graduate school.

    This chaplain had underestimated their burnout scores:
    Personal Accomplishment (PA)—2.
    Emotional Exhaustion (EE)—8.

- Both chaplains (P16 and P20) found their final FBI scores had eased:

  P16's final FBI scores:
  Personal Accomplishment (PA)—5.
  Emotional Exhaustion (EE)—6.
  *Note: This participant left the chaplaincy
  by the end of the study.*

  P20's final FBI scores:
  Personal Accomplishment (PA)—4.
  Emotional Exhaustion (EE)—5.
  *Note: This participant cut back on chaplaincy
  and work commitments to ease their burnout
  and remained an active chaplain.*

- Two chaplains (P8 and P15) indicated the third and fourth highest levels of burnout initially but exhibited the most drastic improvements in their scores by the second FBI.

- Chaplain P25 was the only chaplain in the study whose scores had decreased in PA and increased in EE by the end of the study. *Note: This chaplain expressed that the low ministry connection with both officers and the community influenced their ultimate decision to leave chaplaincy for a ministry that would provide better connection.*

Items of Interest:

- Had no connection with a sending source or denomination—4 (of these 5).

- Had any formal ministry education—1 (P20).

- Had served in church leadership (as a church elder) and reported a strong connection with their church leadership—1 (P15).

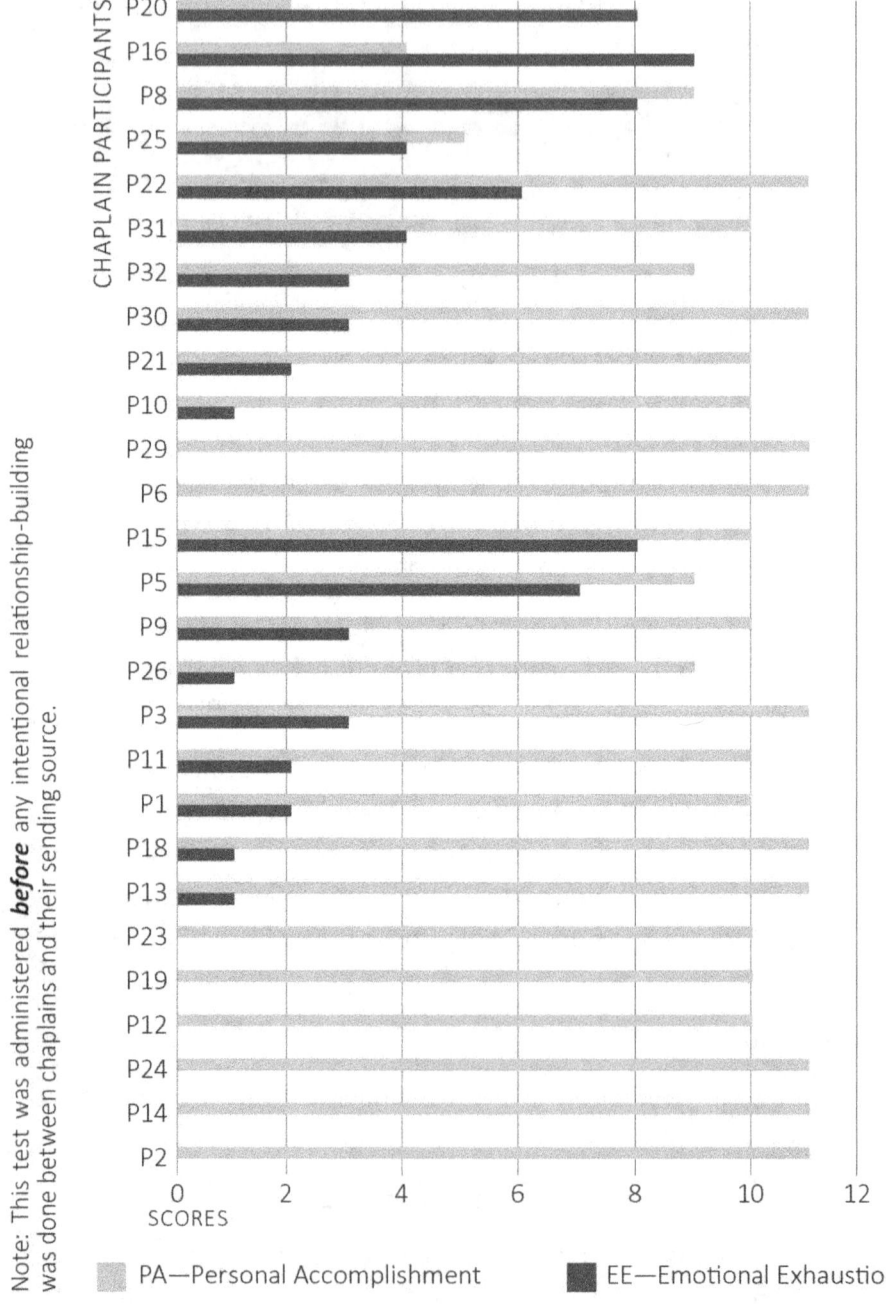

FBI BURNOUT SCORES
27 Chaplain Participants: February 2021

CHAPLAIN PARTICIPANTS

Note: This test was administered *before* any intentional relationship-building was done between chaplains and their sending source.

SCORES

PA—Personal Accomplishment   EE—Emotional Exhaustion

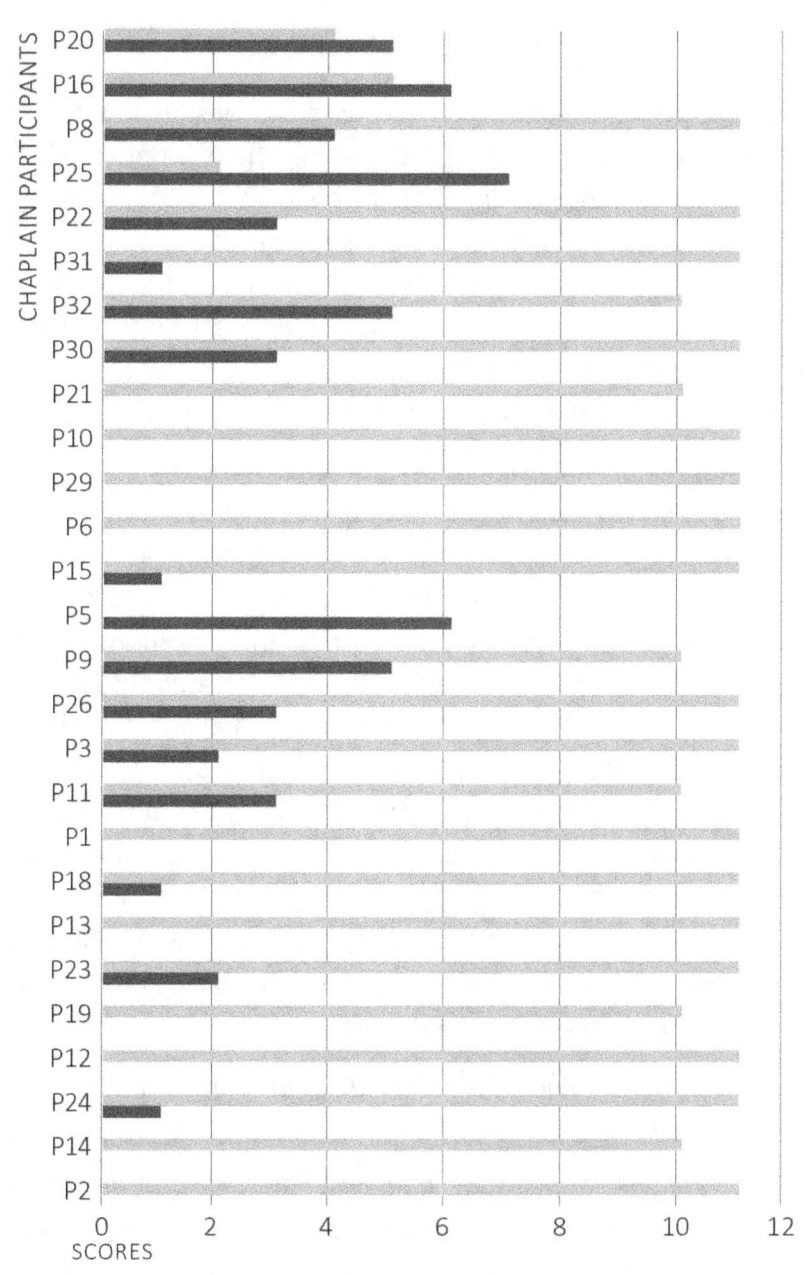

FBI BURNOUT SCORES
27 Chaplain Participants: April 2021

CHAPLAIN PARTICIPANTS

P20, P16, P8, P25, P22, P31, P32, P30, P21, P10, P29, P6, P15, P5, P9, P26, P3, P11, P1, P18, P13, P23, P19, P12, P24, P14, P2

SCORES: 0, 2, 4, 6, 8, 10, 12

PA—Personal Accomplishment   EE—Emotional Exhaustion

Note: This test was administered *after* intentional relationship-building was done between chaplains and their sending source.

WHAT DOES IT MEAN?

If you've struggled to get through the last pages of statistical breakdowns, or if you just skipped to this point, you may be wondering what all this means. First, I found it very hard to conduct a human subject study and pare everything down to simple statements of causation. Humans are incredibly complex. Many factors contribute to burnout, so the conclusions in my study required qualitative interviews to expose what the quantitative testing could not say. Here are some of the other factors that contributed to burnout that chaplains identified in their interviews:

1. COVID was mentioned several times. While many pastors (not in this study) experienced a decrease in their burnout symptoms because they weren't under the massive pressures of Sunday morning services, chaplains' jobs often got harder. Restrictions on in-person ministry, both with the community and at fire stations and police departments, created great stress for chaplains. After all, it is emotionally taxing to perform death notifications by phone or video when you know you will not be able to provide the face-to-face comfort the ministry requires. On top of that, agencies applied the same restrictions to pastoral care for cops and firefighters, largely restricting chaplains from the workplace and ride-alongs. They were almost completely severed from the joy of helping the very people God had called them to. As one chaplain put it:

   "I feel drained, more in a guilty fashion, because I'm not able to—the Department won't let me do—the things I did in the past. I've had very few calls, and mostly I've been handling them by telephone … I don't know what I should know just by looking at the people and getting a feel of what's going on in the situation."

2. Chaplains are often part-time ministers who work full-time jobs in addition to their ministries. Trying to balance both, along with family commitments, impacts their stress levels.

3. Some chaplains entered their ministry with previous trauma that left them with PTSD. On-the-job traumas in chaplaincy can trigger PTSD symptoms and deplete their emotional resources.

4. Women in chaplaincy often face the challenge of acceptance within their ministries from their church leadership. This limits the amount of support they can expect from their church. Eight of the chaplains in this study were women. One of the women explained her situation well:

   "They're not putting roadblocks up to me, but there's not really an acknowledgment there, either. I don't need that. I get it from Jesus."

5. The socio-political environment in the nation during this study was a drain on police chaplains. The George Floyd incident had led to riots and calls to defund the police. Budget cuts sliced into staffing, and police department morale was down across the board.

Many more influences in the complex life events surrounding ministry could make the list. However, the most striking of those noted in the study was the support and affirmation that chaplains receive for their call. The female chaplain quoted above recognized that she gets her affirmation from Jesus; however, we are social creatures. We are made to live and work in community. The minister must have church support to

WE ARE SOCIAL CREATURES—WE ARE MADE TO LIVE AND WORK IN COMMUNITY.

sustain the emotional fortitude needed to endure the trials of ministry. The church is often a key factor in upholding the minister's sense of personal accomplishment. One chaplain said that the study had helped grow her relationship with her pastor and church recognition of her ministry, adding, "but there can always be more."

AFFIRMATION OF CHURCH LEADERS

The affirmation of church leadership is an important theme, especially among those chaplains who self-reported burnout and did not feel connected to their sending source or its leadership. Even tenured chaplains have experienced disconnection with their church leadership, especially when a new pastor takes over that does not maintain continuity in chaplaincy ministry focus. One tenured FRC offered:

> *"My (original pastor) gave me the title of Emergency Care Pastor. It worked really well because I was tied in with the work of the church. But then another pastor came in and (my position) just disappeared. The new pastor knew who I was and just kind of swept me out the door so that my ministry was out in the street where he thought I was supposed to be. The denomination is behind me 100%, but the lead pastor is within my congregation. I used to be invited to the inner sanctum, even to the staff meetings, but not anymore."*

Several other chaplains experienced this phenomenon. One expressed that her previous pastor had commissioned her in a service with prayer and the laying on of hands. However, a new pastor took over that was neither understanding nor supportive of chaplaincy ministry. That pastor did not respond to requests for a meeting during the study, either from his chaplain, who was also a long-time congregant, or from me.

Another chaplain stated that when she took over the ministry a previous chaplain had established, with the pastor's blessing and as a ministry of the church, the pastor changed the status of her ministry to "community service." She felt like she had been downgraded. Yet another chaplain noted regarding the lack of affirmation from his leadership:

"I don't think they know anything. You know, they know that I do this, but we haven't sat down, and I don't think they have an understanding of what I do or why, or how it impacts me."

Many participants underscored the importance of leadership affirmation of their ministry. One chaplain expressed that she now sees how important that affirmation is:

"I'm excited about the opportunity just to try. It's also an excuse for my church to hear more about what we're doing. I don't think that they're as involved as they should be because I think they just think it's all handled. It's all handled, but, you know, (it isn't) really."

A chaplain with a good relationship with her pastor stated that she was called out late one night and sat with a family at a homicide scene for about six hours. She texted her pastor before the call, then showed up at the Sunday morning service immediately after she left the family. She almost fell asleep in the service. When the pastor noticed her head nodding, he acknowledged in front of the congregation what she had been through earlier in the morning. She stated that his affirmation was a great boost to her sense of calling.

One of the tenured chaplains shared his feelings on the caring support of his church leadership and the church body:

"If I did not have my senior pastor, elders, and other members of the congregation—if they did not have the kind of sympathy and empathy, and check in on me, understanding that I'm engaging in difficult work out there and say, 'How can I help you? Make sure you take care of yourself.' [If I did not have] their love and support, boy, I probably couldn't do it. Just knowing that I've got this team of people who really love and support me and recognize it's difficult—it is eminently valuable. In a word, I'd say it's critical. Without the support of my church, I could not do this job."

FORMAL CEREMONIAL "SENDING"

One of the emphases of the study was the importance of the minister's perception that they had been "sent." Again, it is not the purpose of this book to establish a theology of ordination or commissioning. Still, whatever it consists of for your tradition, fasting and prayer, the laying on of hands, the prophetic conferral of ministerial unction—as part of a formal ceremony—all have strong roots in both the Old and New Testaments. Deacons were ordained in the church.[7] Pastors were ordained in each Cretan city.[8] Elders were ordained in each Galatian church.[9] While the prophets and teachers of Antioch were serving and fasting, "... the Holy Spirit said to them, 'Set Barnabas and Saul apart for Me for the work to which I have called them.' Then, when they had fasted, prayed, and laid their hands on them, they sent them away."[10] The following verse says, "So, being sent out by the Holy Spirit ..." indicating that the call of God is confirmed by the response of the Church and subsequently empowered by the Spirit of God.

The Early Church saw fit to ceremonially send those who were called into specific ministries. Most chaplains in the study did not receive a formal ceremony affirming their chaplaincy ministry. Many had already been formally affirmed by ordination or licensing for pastoral ministry. For many, chaplaincy was added to the pulpit ministry, which was their first calling. While these factors did not make them immune to the effects of burnout, they did tend to serve as buffers to burnout. Their church's affirmation worked as an insulating factor.

As previously noted, only three of the ten chaplains who self-identified as experiencing burnout in their ministries had received formal ceremonies upon entering the ministry. Conversely, fourteen of the seventeen chaplains who self-identified as experiencing no burnout in their ministries had received some form of ceremony, whether for their pastoral ordination or for entry into FR chaplaincy. The difference between those who were affirmed by their churches and those who were not is remarkable.

	No Ceremony	Ceremony
Self-Identified Burnout	7	3
No Burnout	3	14

One of the three chaplains among those who had not received a ceremony stated that he could see value in being ecclesiastically commissioned. He added:

"When I talk to people who have been through a ceremony where they have been ordained or commissioned, they don't forget the day. They remember what happened and who was there. I've thought back on it, and I don't feel like I was short-

*changed by my church the way I was sent, but I think back on
some of those people who have that recollection of that day,
and I think how awesome it is to have that, at least. I would
love to go back in time and have somebody at (my agency)
give me this tool to take to my church and my pastor and say,
"This is actually what I want. I want to have a service, just like
when we brought you in. I want to have a service to send me
out. It's kind of a rock to stand on, an altar that was built, a
day they can look back on to say, 'I was sent.'"*

Another chaplain reflected upon the fact that in his denomination, "hospital chaplains are sent with ordinations, degrees, and ceremonies." He wondered why there had been no such sending ceremony or qualification requirements for him when he became a first responder chaplain. Some chaplains revel in the smaller ceremonies they receive, as one did whose pastor offered a prayer of blessing and encouragement, just the two of them in the pastor's office, to send him into chaplaincy. A chaplain who had no church sending source said that the department for whom he works held a pinning ceremony for him that was very affirming. One whose pastor had previously served first responders offered him a private commissioning prayer. He added, "We never did a ceremony. I think that would've been good. I think I would appreciate that."

Another first responder chaplain emphasized the importance of formal ceremonies in his denominational tradition:

*"We had services for all my various ordinations, but it was
very important to them (my denominational leadership)
to make sure that my call to that role in the church did not
abrogate in any way God's call on my life to be a chaplain. I*

really appreciated that. That was something I asked for. That was something they came up with and it kind of cemented that I'm heading in the direction I'm supposed to be heading, and I'm being affirmed not just to be a (pulpit) minister, necessarily, but also that they recognize God's call in my life to be a chaplain."

Several ordained chaplains noted that their ordination was a large, formal, impactful event. However, they each stated that their churches provided no affirming event for their entry into chaplaincy. Extolling the benefits of a formal ceremony, one chaplain stated:

"I think the more structure you can put to it, and the more honor you can put to it, it creates a higher bar of behavior and standards, and an expectation within the community that I think would be helpful to the community."

A strong theology of ministry is applied to pastoral ministry. Yet many church leaders fail to develop a theology of chaplaincy that includes the "why" and "how" relating to sending chaplains from their churches into their various ministries. Ceremonies are very seldom considered for chaplain commissioning in many churches. Pastors put more thought and effort into child baptisms or dedications than on purposefully and publicly anointing their chaplains for their work. One tenured chaplain explained his theological view on commissioning chaplains for ministry:

"I like to use the term anointing, which is very much an Old Testament concept. When someone was commissioned to go out and do the Lord's work, they went through a process, literally a physical anointing with oil. It still was a spiritual anointing from God to go out and do the work. And then, of

course, it's interesting that when Jesus sent out the 70, He didn't do it by the concept of an anointing, but it was almost as if this was the first example of a true, Holy Spirit anointing and commissioning by Jesus, speaking with authority when He sent them out. I really look at being commissioned as a chaplain with the Old Testament concept of having an anointing from the Lord for the work."

The importance of calling is essential, but it is only one-half of the equation. It is a very important piece. The church can get it wrong and send someone they hasten to lay hands on, someone who presents as charismatic and a good fit for ministry. However, the rigorous process of examining and confirming a call to ministry must include affirming action by the sending church. Anyone sent into ministry ought to be able to look back on the day the Body of Christ recognized and anointed them for a specific ministry to a particular people. They must be able to recall that day, especially when the joy of ministry suddenly requires laborious effort, when pressures and persecutions arise. They must also know they have the ongoing support of that church.

ANYONE SENT INTO MINISTRY OUGHT TO BE ABLE TO LOOK BACK ON THE DAY THE BODY OF CHRIST RECOGNIZED AND ANOINTED THEM FOR A SPECIFIC MINISTRY TO A PARTICULAR PEOPLE.

REFLECTION

*"Do not neglect the spiritual gift within you, which
was granted to you through words of prophecy with
the laying on of hands by the council of elders."*
1 TIMOTHY 4:14

Consider your calling. Perhaps you were ordained in a large ceremony that included prayer, worship, and the laying on of hands. I received a stole and shepherd's crook in a worship service where a couple of dozen pastors were ordained before several thousand supporters. It was incredibly affirming. The powerful prayer of my pastor, who laid his hands upon my head, carried a deep spiritual unction that I remember to this day.

- Think back to when you first recognized God's call to ministry. What made that clear? Can you remember how you felt or what it was that confirmed the call was from Him and compelled you to say yes? Reflect on this now and let that memory encourage you.

- If you have not been recognized in your ministry through a singular, Spirit-led event, I am sorry. Whether this has bothered you for some time or if, while reading this chapter, it has pricked you and caused you to feel pain or rejection, I am sorry. Whether you are a chaplain, elder, deacon, or perhaps you are a woman performing ministry tasks in one of these roles without formal recognition or commission, whatever the case may be, the affirmation of those you labor among is crucial. Yes, affirmation comes from God. It should also come from your church leadership.

If this describes you, I encourage you to take a moment to email or call your pastor or a trusted church elder. Set an appointment with them. Get on their calendar. Speak with them about the church's formal recognition of your ministry—and what they might require.

- If you have been formally ordained or recognized, take a moment to reflect on that event and its spiritual significance for your ministry. Perhaps you can reach out to those who were part of that experience and thank them for their support.

- Ask the Lord to refresh your spirit and fill you again with His. Let this be a moment of renewal of commitment to your call.

PRAYER OF ENCOURAGEMENT

Father, I thank You for the call to shepherd Your people. Thank You for choosing me and setting me apart for Your service. I do not take this lightly. It is much more than a career choice; it is a response to my deep love for You and out of gratitude for all You have done for me. Being anointed as a minister of the Gospel—bringing good news to the poor, proclaiming release to captives and recovery of sight to the blind, setting free those who are oppressed,[11] binding up the brokenhearted, comforting those who mourn, and giving them a garland instead of ashes, the oil of gladness instead of mourning, and the cloak of praise instead of a disheartened spirit[12]—this is a sacred call.

I rely upon Your strength and grace to walk in this calling, and I ask You to surround me with and connect me to fellow ministers who share this mantle and carry this burden. Thank You that I am not alone, I labor among many, and the weight is shared. The glory is Yours. Guide me in all that I say and do, and help me to follow Your command to love others as You have loved me. In Christ Jesus, amen.

ENDNOTES

1 The Church has abused the title of *pastor*. My theology of eldership includes each of the five-fold gifts of Christ to the Church; apostles, prophets, evangelists, pastors, and teachers, or more correctly, pastor-teachers. You will find them represented in our churches and evidenced by their expressions of leadership and calling. You certainly do not need to agree with my theology on this matter. However, since we have come to use the title of pastor for all the offices, I do so in this book to avoid confusion.

2 1 Peter 5:1-4.

3 Christopher J. Adams, et al., "Clergy Burnout: A Comparison Study with Other Helping Professions," *Pastoral Psychology* 66, no. 2 (04, 2017): 168.

4 1 Timothy 3:1.

5 1 Timothy 5:22.

6 "Sending source" is a moniker I used to denote local churches, denominations, or other endorsers who "send" chaplains into the field. To send a minister requires some affirmation of their ministry, including theological training, oversight, ordination, or certification. Military, hospital, hospice, and VA chaplains have extensive requirements, most often including a master's degree and ordination, as do many denominational pastors. The accessioning of a chaplain in less-organized ministries, like first responder chaplains, is sometimes as informal as a chief recognizing bold faith in one of his cops or firefighters and asking them to be their chaplain.

7 Acts 6:1-6.

8 Titus 1:5.

9 Acts 14:23.

10 Acts 13:2-3.

11 See Luke 4:18; Isaiah 61:1-2.

12 See Isaiah 61:3.

CHAPTER NINE
ONGOING SUPPORT

"You yourselves also know, Philippians, that at the first preaching of the gospel, after I left Macedonia, no church shared with me in the matter of giving and receiving except you alone; for even in Thessalonica you sent a gift more than once for my needs."[1]

"Many clergy appear to be people-pleasers by nature; when their work does not go well and the congregation does not provide social support, these clergy may react by becoming cynical and isolating themselves from church members, family, and peers."[2]

SUPPORT IS ESSENTIAL

The affirmation of the church is not just a fire-and-forget weapon. A responsible church does not just send people out into the field and then erase their names from the membership rolls. They add them to their ministry staff, put them on prayer lists, provide material support, offer supervision and church training, and monitor their well-being. In other words, when a church formally commissions a minister, they are more likely to look at the minister's work as a part of the church ministry portfolio. Hopefully, the church also cultivates a relational connection with that minister along the way.

ISOLATION IS A MINISTRY DESTROYER. YOUR SENDING CHURCH SHOULD BE YOUR PRIMARY SOCIAL NETWORK FOR YOUR SPIRITUAL GUIDANCE AND GROWTH.

Conversely, as a minister commissioned by a church, you have an obligation to remain in relationship with them, as well. You must stay connected to that sending source. You should report back on your ministry to an assigned member of church leadership, and you should be in fellowship at the church's services whenever possible. You are a missionary, but you are local. You need the Body of Christ, and it needs to honor its connection to you. Isolation is a ministry destroyer. Your sending church should be your primary social network for your spiritual guidance and growth.

In a profession with so many inherent challenges that are often faced without the support and nurturance of a well-established social network of trusted people, it is not surprising that clergy often find themselves exhausted, depleted, and languishing in the throes of burnout. Research has shown that the presence of a well-established system of support is related to lower levels of burnout while, conversely, a lack of social support is linked to increased burnout.[3]

Healthy connections like this can be difficult for foreign missionaries and military chaplains. Missionaries are, by nature, far removed from their home church. They are usually connected with many churches, perhaps through the denomination they serve. They may start a church in the city where they minister, or they may attend one. They may go as covert ministers, knowing the country they are in does not approve of Christian ministry within their borders. Yet missionaries, too, must find ways to be connected to the Body of Christ for more than just funding for their work.

Military chaplains are moved about frequently. They often lose touch with their home churches. They tend to tie in with their denominational endorser, but only have rare opportunities for fellowship within their tradition, perhaps once per year at a chaplain or ministers' conference. Their denomination may not be represented near their next duty station. On deployments, they may become the sole local representative of their denomination, or even of the Christian faith, on their assigned base or region. Thus, they often build close ties with chaplains of other denominations. This type of inter-denominational fellowship is unique to missionaries in the field as well as to many chaplaincy types, such as first responder, hospital, and institutional chaplaincies.

One of the difficulties military chaplains can face is isolation. During a combat deployment, for instance, a chaplain may be out at sea or at a FOB (forward operating base), completely isolated from other chaplains. Letters, phone calls, and video conferencing may or may not be available consistently. Care packages can be few and far between. Though the connections these chaplains have built will be put on hold, knowing they are connected provides another anchor for the soul.

As a pastor, I focused on building relationships with just a few missionaries rather than trying to support all that our church could. We sent eleven of the twenty people from our church plant on a trip to visit our missionaries in Northern Asia in just our second year. We sent a team of seven to Tanzania to support missionaries there, and I traveled solo to each country to show my support for them. I wanted them to know that even though we weren't their home church, they were connected back home. They needed the encouragement of knowing that many held them close in their thoughts and prayers. I wanted to show them they were a priority to us.

We also supported each of our missionaries with large donations compared to our church size. We didn't want to be a church a missionary had to feel indebted to for fifty dollars per month, just so we could brag about a broad missions catalog. We wanted our support to be meaningful. Our church always valued generosity, so giving—and giving well—was always a top priority. A church that skimps on the support it provides missionaries and other ministries shows those they send that they are valued only enough to check a box in their portfolio.

Missionaries, chaplains, food bank directors, homelessness outreaches, and evangelists need to know that they are not forgotten, whether they operate across the street or across the ocean. They are not left to their own devices. They have people they can lean on who know them by name and will answer the phone when they call. One chaplain shared this about their pastor: "Since the first FBI, I have thought about my lead pastor as a send[ing] source. He is silent to all I do or wish to do. It frustrates me because I don't trust he would empathize or change his time for me."

This is not how it should be for anyone, much less God's shepherds. Pastors, please evaluate the kind of support you give to these valuable front-line ministers. As you read the next section, I hope to encourage you to empower others and grow your outreach well beyond your church walls.

HOW PASTORS VIEW CHAPLAINS

I was a senior pastor for sixteen years, so I understand and empathize with how demanding pastoral duties are. You have so much on your plate that it seems unfair to ask you to divert attention to other ministries. However, your calling is not only to the people within your church. Paul reminds us that our ministry is "for the equipping of the saints for the work of ministry, for the building up of the body of Christ."[4] Please consider how important it is to fully equip your church members to **do** ministry, not just to **receive** it.

As I have noted, formally licensed pulpit ministers have often seen chaplains as something less than pastors. Mark Newitt puts it in brutal terms regarding hospital chaplains and their relationship with the church, noting that it is "characterized by a deep sense of alienation in one direction and profound mistrust in the other."[5] Part of this phenomenon within the ministerial culture is likely due to the chaplain's primary work finding its locus outside of the church walls and among largely unchurched populations.

Though the church sends missionaries overseas in settings among the unchurched, while it sends chaplains merely across town, missionaries receive the full warrant of the church to bring the Gospel to the nations. Churches view foreign missionaries as fulfilling the Great Commission, yet they do not as readily acknowledge local missionaries, like chaplains, as doing the same. They sometimes treat first responder missions as something that falls short of the Great Commission. Nothing could be further from the truth.

The first responder chaplain's vocation, as well as that of military and hospital chaplains, shapes who they are and how Christians often perceive them. This impacts how the church at large receives them, as well. Many churches are generally ignorant of what chaplains do, while others are acquainted with them only in the context of the military, prisons, and hospitals. Most are unaware that chaplains serve in community settings—not just police and fire departments—but also casinos, airports, and racetracks, among many other locations one might not expect to find a minister of God "on the job."

There is often an air of discomfort in the church with such secular institutions, some of which Christians see as "the belly of the beast," and an equal discomfort with the idea of sending Christian ministers into those places.[6] George Barna has identified a link showing that despite this discomfort, a growing number of people who practice their faith outside of the institutional church claim to have an individualized relationship with Jesus over and against His church. They prefer to discuss issues of faith within the context of personal relationships apart from religious events or institutions.[7]

This is telling.

I am not endorsing this idea as healthy but rather pointing out that there is a mission field in that group to which someone must be sent. These Christian exiles and secular settings require someone who is theologically equipped not only to be an apologist for Christ and the church but also to provide Christian ministrations to them. They may be wandering, disaffected, or discouraged with their church experience, but they still need

> **THEY MAY BE WANDERING, DISAFFECTED, OR DISCOURAGED WITH THEIR CHURCH EXPERIENCE, BUT THEY STILL NEED COMMUNION, BAPTISM, BIBLICAL TRAINING, PRAYER, COUNSELING, AND CONSOLATION.**

communion, baptism, biblical training, prayer, counseling, and consolation. Chaplains are uniquely situated to provide ministry to those Christians you may never see enter your church doors. And the lost in those venues may never see a Christian witness in their worlds without the presence of a chaplain.

These ministers, along with others you are involved in sending, need your mentorship, guidance, equipping (both substantive and sacred), oversight, spiritual training, and relational connection. If you cannot do it yourself—and I am not suggesting that you can—provide them with someone from your church who can. Assign a deacon or elder in your ministry to be their contact person—not a passive contact, but an active contact with whom they can meet and perhaps connect at a deeper level. Give them time to share their ministry with the church. Put them in your daily or weekly prayer list. Put their picture on your website and your missions map. Take ownership of their mission efforts as your church's cherished ministry arm.

HOW DID PASTORS IN THE STUDY VIEW CHAPLAINCY?

As I met with pastors and their chaplains in the study, the questions posed encouraged discussion around their understanding of the theology of first responder chaplain ministry and pastoral relationships with their chaplains. However, few of the sending churches expressed initial forethought about a theology of chaplaincy ministry. Instead, most subsumed their understanding of chaplaincy under the umbrella category of pastoral or foreign missions ministries.

One denominational representative, whose job it was specifically to track its ordained and licensed ministers, shared the most cogent, predefined theology of ministry outside of the walls of the church:

"In the theology of Paul, we could bring out that you believe in the whole work of the church. This is one of our affirmations. Or another way to say it is the whole work of the Gospel— that it's not just about personal life transformation that might be associated with a minister's work for a church or as an evangelist, but we also know that it's about community transformation. It's about what Jesus taught us to pray for His Kingdom to be established here on Earth as it is in heaven.[8] We know whether it be [ministering to a] first responder, or sitting by a bedside in a hospital, or out on the battlefield in Iraq, it is part of the trajectory of the Gospel. It's not specifically written down, 'This is what we believe is our theology for First Responders.' It is the whole work of the church or the whole work of the Gospel."

Another pastor gave an off-the-cuff response that indicated the same approach to ministry outside of the church walls:

"We're called for radical engagement and to pray for the peace of the city, to work for the prosperity and the peace and the good of the broader community in which we are a radical sub-community.[9] We are Christ to the city, and I really love [the chaplain's] own thinking about how he is, in some sense, a pastor of our city and does that pastoring through his chaplaincy work."

Most of the pastors in the study recognized the nature of chaplaincy work as a local mission in which the chaplains are not always permitted to present or preach the Gospel outright but rather to be the hands and feet of Christ. They referenced the need to "love the Lord your God with all your heart, and with all your soul, and with all your strength, and with all your mind; and your neighbor as yourself."[10] One pastor spoke of the offices of the church from Ephesians 4:11, noting that, while his church recognizes their chaplain as an elder, he sees his own ministry as one containing the office ministries of apostle and evangelist.

Other pastors expressed a similar understanding of the first responder chaplain's role as evangelistic in nature, even though they may not always overtly preach the Gospel. They agreed that serving the community in times of crisis among those who are suffering is a way to express love for God by loving their neighbors. One pastor referenced John 17:15 and 18, where Jesus prayed, "I am not asking You to take them out of the world, but to keep them away from the evil one.… Just as You sent Me into the world, I also sent them into the world." He emphasized the incarnational nature of chaplaincy, just as another pastor expressed:

> *"Jesus deeply understands our pain. We need people that have that experience, training, and understanding to be able to come alongside them. Not only are they first responders in the sense that they hear about it first, but they have that training and that Christlikeness to be able to walk with people in their pain."*

There was no unanimity in how to describe the role of the chaplain regarding biblical titles. Pastors variously referred to them as missionaries, pastors, evangelists, apostles, and elders, or simply as laypersons fulfilling the biblical vision of a priesthood of all believers. Very few indicated that they would require ordination for the role of the chaplain, many preferring to defer to the requirements of the agencies the chaplains serve.

Three of the pastors indicated that ordination, or at minimum a license, would be required for their organization to endorse a chaplain for ministry. However, only one reduced chaplaincy ministry to a lay ministry that did not need recognition from the church, whether at a local or denominational level. The three pastors requiring ordination also required a master's degree: either a master's of divinity or a general ministry master's. One of the three also required four units of Clinical Pastoral Education and an intent to become a board-certified chaplain.

Overall, the remainder of the pastors had developed vague standards, none of which had been codified in their church operations manuals. Many pastors stated that they had not thought through the requirements for commissioning chaplains, as they had never commissioned a first responder chaplain prior to the one they now endorsed. Many expressed that their participation in the study had, as one put it, "shone a bright light on something I think is a challenge, which is the general, loose understanding of what (first responder) chaplaincy is all about."

This theme permeated the pastoral discussions. Most of the pastors had only minimal exposure to first responder ministries, and only one had been a first responder chaplain previously. Another had responded to callouts in his capacity as a pastor, while another was the head of a chaplaincy organizational agency. The remaining sending source representatives expressed that they knew little of what police and fire chaplains did, although many had heard stories of trauma from their own chaplains. One pastor summed it up this way:

> *"It might be nice to have a little bit more of an understanding of what goes on in training. [My chaplain] shared with me a little bit about her experience, but I didn't have an extensive understanding of what it was she was doing."*

THE LINK BETWEEN MINISTRY BURNOUT
AND HEALTHY CONNECTION

As chapter eight exposed, the study revealed a distinct difference in burnout rates between those chaplains who had excellent relationships with their pastors or church leaders and those who had little or no connection to anyone in their church's leadership. One quote from my study chaplains about their pastor haunts me: "He is silent to all I do or wish to do." It was striking to me that only eleven pastors of twenty-three possible actually took the time to engage with their chaplain and me in conversation—twelve did not respond.

A terrible witness to pastoral care was revealed in the fact that several pastors never even responded to their chaplains' calls or emails, much less mine. One chaplain indicated that she knew her pastor just did not have time to participate in the study. If these statements are true, how is it that no one else in church leadership was mature enough and available to the chaplain to support them in their ministry?

I admit that I was a little hard on pastors in the study. I was disappointed in those who, as the overseers of their church, did not seem to have an awareness that such ministry efforts deserve either their time or their delegation of ministry oversight to someone who has time. As a pastor, I knew I could not do everything that tugged at my time. However, developing leaders who could take on tasks I could not engage in was essential. The low interaction from the pastors in the study was unexpected. Clearly, there is much room for increasing awareness and even some growth here.

Thankfully, the study also revealed many healthy and effective relationships between church leadership and chaplains. The best examples included churches that saw their chaplains as a vital outreach ministry to their community and honored them as such. Many included a pastor-chaplain association that was a deep, well-built relationship. They were friends, confidants, and co-equals in ministry. That kind of relationship takes time, but it is also healing and healthy for a pastor to have another minister alongside them with whom they can build enough trust to share their own struggles and joys.

As pastors, we tend to get reduced to running the treadmill in ministry. So understand that I am not asking you to take on yet another ministry task. However, the ministries you support deserve more than a brief note to a fire or police department that says, "Yeah, sure. They're okay. They won't hurt anyone. Let them do that chaplain thing."

IF YOU SEND OUT A MINISTER WITHOUT A CONNECTION TO YOUR LEADERSHIP, YOU ARE SENDING THEM INTO THE PATH OF BURNOUT.

If you send out a minister without a connection to your leadership, you are sending them into the path of burnout.

Support them.

Honor them as co-laborers in Christ.

Ensure they are theologically trained and meet the requirements for your church or denomination for pastoral ministry because they will be doing just that.

Lay hands on them. Pray over them. Commission them. Send them.

BECOMING A CHAPLAIN

In the Army, we used to remind younger soldiers that no one would care for their careers for them. Their advancement, training, and record-keeping were their responsibility. The same goes for chaplains.

I spent a full chapter encouraging you to consider your callings—both to the chaplaincy and to the church in which you seek recognition for it. Very few pastors are recruiting chaplains for any position, much less the one to which you feel called. You will likely have to pioneer your path.

Pastors are pulled from many directions by their many duties within the church. The larger the church, the greater the responsibilities and (hopefully) the staff size. You cannot just walk around hoping someone has a vision from God that you are to be commissioned as a chaplain and prophesy to the pastor and his staff for you. That is a fine hope, but we had a saying in the Army: "Hope is not a method."

Here are some practical suggestions:

- I strongly recommend you set an appointment with your pastor, or someone on the pastoral staff, to talk about your ministry ambitions.

- Do some research in advance to find out what it takes to become a chaplain in your local area, depending upon where you wish to minister.

- Make sure you know your church or denominational requirements for attaining the appropriate ministry status to become a chaplain.

- The main thing, however, is to get a foot in the pastor's door to share your specific sense of calling. Tell them you want to begin whatever process is required to fulfill that call.

- Finally, be like Jacob, and don't let go until you are blessed!

Be persistent. If your vision for ministry is based on a true calling from God, it is worth fighting for. However, that doesn't mean simply demanding others recognize it. You may have to follow the advice of

Paul: "Be diligent to present yourself approved to God as a worker who does not need to be ashamed, accurately handling the word of truth."[11] This means that you should be amenable to the educational, doctrinal, and lifestyle requirements of the church or denomination in which you were called. Most of all, seek to be filled with the Spirit, that your ministry might not be found "in persuasive words of wisdom, but in demonstration of the Spirit and of power."[12]

You owe those to whom you speak not a good conversation with a smart chaplain, but an encounter with God.

You should also check to see if you have any Chaplaincy Organizational Agencies in your area. (See the next section for a more complete discussion about COAs.) They may be formal organizations or loose fellowships. They will often cater specifically to your chosen chaplaincy field. If your field is unique, such as a private school or race car chaplaincy, there may be a national organization that can help guide you. If the organization you seek to serve is a large police or fire department or hospital, they will have a lead chaplain with whom you can speak for guidance. Proverbs 15:22 is instructive:

> **"Without consultation, plans are frustrated,**
> **But with many counselors they succeed."**

Find other chaplains in your desired field and ask them every question you can about what it takes to get where they are. I have found that an ample amount of coffee and donuts often keep the conversation lively with chaplains.

The greatest evidence of a mistaken calling is an unwillingness to endure the requisite process to meet the requirements for becoming a minister of God. That comes from pride or slothfulness. However, a diligent pursuit of God's presence in your life, along with a teachable spirit and good study habits, will bring success in fulfilling His calling. It will also put you in a good place to avoid burning out early. The chaplains in the study ranged from the early thirties to the mid-seventies. However, there were only three under the age of fifty, and two of those were burning out. As I advised before, do not be impatient. God will unfold His work in you in His time.

Understand that the reason many pastors are unsure about chaplains is that many do not wish to pursue the same training and experience that pastors themselves must. When Paul told Timothy not to lay hands on anyone quickly, he was talking about just that. Don't be that guy (or gal). Don't be the one who is demanding recognition without humbly working for it and putting in the time and effort. Chaplaincy requires the ability to work independently, which demands maturity. If you demonstrate that to a pastor, they are much more likely to support you—and that will (again) help you enjoy a long, burnout-free ministry.

MANY PASTORS ARE UNSURE ABOUT CHAPLAINS BECAUSE MANY CHAPLAINS DO NOT WISH TO PURSUE THE SAME TRAINING AND EXPERIENCE THAT PASTORS THEMSELVES MUST.

CHAPLAINCY ORGANIZATIONAL AGENCIES

The world of police and fire chaplaincy is quickly organizing and establishing itself as a professional ministry. Police and fire agencies are starting to demand professional credentialing for their chaplains to limit their liability and ensure their employees get the best, most qualified ministers available. The days of handing out badges to people without the backing of legitimate credentialing agencies are numbered. In time, this will also bleed over into other less formal chaplaincy sectors.

The number of Chaplaincy Organizational Agencies (COAs) is rising as the need for accountability and training becomes standardized. The agency I worked with as a police chaplain, the Tacoma-Pierce County Chaplaincy (TPCC), is one such agency. These COAs typically do not ordain or endorse chaplains but provide a source of ministerial legitimacy for the chaplains the local agencies they serve utilize in their departments.

It is important to note that COAs do not replace the church as the source for a chaplain's theological training, ministerial credentialing, or personal accountability. TPCC's Board of Directors participated in the study as a voice for COAs and joined a focus group. One board member stated about the chaplain-church relationship:

> *"We rely upon the chaplain's relationship with their church body. We assume that it is robust, that they take the opportunity to grow, that they engage in opportunities to be trained, supported, and encouraged."*

During the focus group, a significant point emerged: the church is largely insulated from governmental regulation compared to other non-profit agencies, like COAs. Thus, two acknowledgments should guide COAs. First, they must recognize that they are not churches and should not try to be like them in function or structure. They cannot legally organize as a church and therefore should, as one board member put it, "stay within its lane." Another member stated:

> *"We are working on strengthening that connection between the chaplains and their church and TPCC to close the loop...to make sure the chaplains are adequately covered and understand that TPCC doesn't exist to replace that relationship."*

Second, as a multi-denominational Christian organization, they must rely upon churches to take on the ecclesial responsibility of preparing their chaplains for ministry according to their denominational doctrines and practices. The board emphasized that they are not a licensing or ordaining body. It is up to churches to provide the theological training and qualification their tradition requires. Too often in the past, some churches provided only a perfunctory pastoral letter of recommendation. This left in question whether pastors truly knew the ministry to which they were sending the chaplain candidate or whether the candidate was fully qualified to conduct chaplaincy ministry. One board member captured it this way after speaking with local pastors:

> *"I had conversations with a lot of our area churches and asked them, 'Hey, if you have sent somebody to TPCC to serve in this mission field, what's your understanding of the relationship that we have with you and that you have with them?'*
>
> *A lot of the pastors had a very consistent message. They said, 'Well, we don't even know really what to expect. We don't even have a good understanding of what they're getting themselves into.'*
>
> *So, I think a lot of it isn't necessarily the level of seriousness that they send them off with, but maybe they think, "This is a 40- to 50-year-old organization that is taking my parishioners under their wing and sending them out in the mission field. I'm good.' That's a big disconnect that I've noticed."*

TPCC's relationship with churches is intended to be one of accountability and support for the chaplain. It ensures that the chaplain maintains a healthy tether to their church. TPCC would not know about the ongoing connection of church and chaplain without being in a relationship with that church or having the chaplain self-report any change in their church membership. A board member further detailed the need for a close chaplain-church tie:

> "If that chaplain was to fall away from what that pastor or church leader perceives to be a positive path of spiritual growth, and they stop seeing them in the pews every Sunday... if things aren't going well in their mind, as far as their participation in the life of the church, we want to know about that because we understand the importance of them being tethered to their church for spiritual growth. Chaplains are out there pouring out into other people's lives quite a bit. They need to be poured into. While TPCC exists to be a support structure, as far as peer support goes, they also get that from their church."

CHAPLAINS ARE OUT THERE POURING OUT INTO OTHER PEOPLE'S LIVES QUITE A BIT— THEY NEED TO BE POURED INTO.

TPCC has watched chaplains spiral downward into dysfunction, only to later discover, after intervening in their ministry struggles, that the chaplain had long since left their sending church altogether. Chaplains may also simply move from one church to another without notifying either the COA or their agency. They may not even let their new church leadership know of their ministry work. Such a situation severs accountability and puts the chaplain in a position where they lack knowledgeable support from key players in their ministry. One board member suggested:

"We might choose once a year as our time to go through and (check to see if) our people are connected to a sending church that has changed, to require them to have that name on file with us."

Pastoral changes within a church can also create a gap in understanding and ecclesiastical covering.

"That incoming pastor has come with a different view of qualifications to go into ministry, or into the mission field, and possibly questions a chaplain fitting into that mold. In those instances, the role of TPCC has been to come around that chaplain and encourage them to serve at a church that's going to support them in their calling."

The board emphasized that spiritual authority in the chaplain's life is most directly located within their sending church. The partnership between TPCC and churches provides necessary support to the agencies chaplains serve. These agencies typically do not have any connection with the sending churches and are often unaware of how churches endorse chaplains for service:

"You have to have the support of the spiritual authority in your life as a Christian. If we had a real problem with a chaplain acting out, it would be nice to have the assistance of the spiritual authority in their life to come alongside, even if we had to remove them. Then it would be done in a biblical way that isn't just 'us versus them,' but the spiritual authority in their life (sic)."

The board expressed its need to keep close relationships with churches while remaining distinct in its primary function and educating churches on theirs. Churches are afforded significant protections under the Constitution in that they cannot be compelled by law to abandon or abrogate their beliefs or practices. Parachurch ministries often face greater legal challenges to faith-based policies and procedures than churches. Remaining close to the greater church culture, particularly by giving churches and denominations control of their chaplains and policies, insulates COAs from lawsuits and other challenges to how they conduct their parachurch ministry.

The TPCC board also spoke to the spiritual importance of encouraging better connections between chaplains and their sending sources, the quality of which is often evidenced by how the chaplains are initially prepared and sent.

> "I've seen some of the sending churches give us a very robust send-off. It's something that they speak directly to as far as the ongoing commitment to the spiritual growth and covering they're going to provide the chaplain."

The church often expresses that commitment by:

> "... the laying on of hands in a ceremony to send them off with that awareness of their covering and blessing."

As the TPCC Director stated,

> "My goal is not to dictate to them what their theology should be, but to help them come up with a better process."

Christian COAs perform a vital duty to both church and chaplain. In a ministry where one can become very isolated from their spiritual source, they often provide better church-chaplain connectivity, chaplain-specific training, and a level of fellowship with other chaplains that is not often easy for chaplains to secure within their church ministry circles. COAs cannot fulfill all the duties of the sending church or denomination, but they can be ministry multipliers by fulfilling the needs of the receiving agencies for qualified, trained chaplains and the needs of churches to remain in relationship with those they send. These are important gaps to fill to reduce the chaplain's likelihood of suffering from isolation-related burnout.

REFLECTION

"Beloved, let us love one another; for love
is from God, and everyone who loves has
been born of God and knows God."

1 JOHN 4:7

I wrote this book to all who have embraced a ministry calling and have found themselves on the treadmill. I have been the pastor of a small church and worked as a chaplain in the Army Reserves and my local police department. I was busy with family, secular work, and too many other things to name. I burned out.

I wrote this book as a warning that burnout is real. Burnout is also avoidable. But even if you fall into its clutches, burnout is recoverable. However, recovery will take a concerted effort on your part to implement strategies that can help you reduce your ongoing burnout risk.

I invite you to reflect on these thoughts:

- We know that love is not self-seeking. How have you loved and connected with the ministers in your sphere of influence?

- Please take account of how you have honored them. How have you upheld their calling to share the Gospel, just as you have been called and as you desire to be honored and supported?

177

- Now, take a moment to pray for their provision, blessing, favor, and success. Most of all, rejoice in their victories so that God may honor you with the same.

- Finally, as you run your race, be sure you do not run so hard that you collapse before the finish line.

PRAYER OF ENCOURAGEMENT

Father, I receive Paul's wise instruction to appreciate those who diligently labor among us and those who have charge over me and give me instruction. Help me get to know them better. Help me to hold them in high esteem and love them well in honor of the work they do. Help me to share the burden of ministry alongside them so that their load may be lightened and their hearts encouraged.

I need meaningful relationships in my life and my ministry. I was not meant to labor alone. Bring those around me who will correct me when I stray, encourage me when I am weary, come alongside me when I am heavy-laden, and patiently counsel me in my frustration. I will not try to do this ministry life alone. I need co-laborers as I cannot do it all alone. I will submit to Your process and guidance in coming under their authority, working peaceably with them to advance Your Kingdom, and leading where You have called me to lead.

I will rejoice always, pray without ceasing, and in everything give thanks, for this is Your will for me in Christ Jesus. Amen.[13]

ENDNOTES

1 Philippians 4:15-16.

2 Richard Wayne Foss, "Burnout among Clergy and Helping Professionals: Situational and Personality Correlates" (Ph.D. diss., Fuller Theological Seminary, 2002), 16.

3 Ryan C. Staley et al., "Strategies Employed by Clergy to Prevent and Cope with Interpersonal Isolation," *Pastoral Psychology* 62, no. 6 (12, 2013): 846.

4 Ephesians 4:12.

5 Mark Newitt, "New Directions in Hospital Chaplaincy: Chaplains – the Church's embedded apologists?" *Theology* 117, no. 6, (2014): 417.

6 Robert Crick, *Outside the Gates: Theology, History, and Practice of Chaplaincy Ministries* (Oviedo, FL: HigherLife Publishing, 2012), 70-71.

7 See George Barna, "Meet Those Who Love Jesus But Not the Church," Research Releases in Faith and Christianity, March 2017, https://www.barna.com/research/meet-love-jesus-not-church/.

8 See Matthew 6:10.

9 See Jeremiah 29:7.

10 Luke 10:27.

11 2 Timothy 2:15.

12 1 Corinthians 2:4b.

13 Prayer adapted from 1 Thessalonians 5:12-18.

"THE PLACE GOD CALLS YOU TO
IS THE PLACE WHERE YOUR DEEP
GLADNESS AND THE WORLD'S
DEEP HUNGER MEET."

—FREDERICK BUECHNER

CHAPTER TEN

FINAL THOUGHTS

"Whoever drinks of the water that I will give him shall never be thirsty; but the water that I will give him will become in him a fountain of water springing up to eternal life."[1]

"Spiritual dryness emerged as the primary predictor of emotional exhaustion, the stress dimension of burnout. Rather than any specific spiritual, rest-taking, or support system practice (i.e., praying, fasting, taking retreats, or meeting with a close friend), this finding reinforces the premise that pastors, by virtue of their calling, need to nurture an ongoing and renewing relationship with God to maintain life balance, reduce stress, and avoid burnout."[2]

WORLDLY TRIALS, HEAVENLY HOPE

In truth, I often look at my burnout story and think of what a crybaby I am. I have endured so little compared to others, yet I so often felt my energy, my hope, and my identity slip far away from my reach. I looked at Scripture and found that others had been through so much more than I had.

Paul detailed his travails, which put mine to shame:

> But in whatever respect anyone else is bold—I am speaking
> in foolishness—I too am bold. Are they Hebrews? So am I. Are
> they Israelites? So am I. Are they descendants of Abraham? So
> am I. Are they servants of Christ? I am speaking as if insane—I
> more so; in far more labors, in far more imprisonments,
> beaten times without number, often in danger of death. Five
> times I received from the Jews thirty-nine lashes. Three times
> I was beaten with rods, once I was stoned, three times I was
> shipwrecked, a night and a day I have spent adrift at sea. I have
> been on frequent journeys, in dangers from rivers, dangers
> from robbers, dangers from my countrymen, dangers from
> the Gentiles, dangers in the city, dangers in the wilderness,
> dangers at sea, dangers among false brothers; I have been in
> labor and hardship, through many sleepless nights, in hunger
> and thirst, often without food, in cold and exposure.[3]

Despite all of these deadly and disheartening trials, Paul turns his focus
not on himself but upon the Church:

> Apart from such external things, there is the daily pressure on
> me of concern for all the churches. Who is weak without my
> being weak? Who is led into sin without my intense concern?[4]

If any man aside from Jesus was a candidate for burnout, it was Paul.
And yet, we never hear of him using the word *burnout* to describe a
point in his ministry when he just kind of lost it. It is easier to identify
with Peter, who denied Jesus three times. Then, after bearing witness
to His resurrection, Peter returned to being a fisherman. Now there

is an example of someone who could be described as experiencing a form of burnout. Perhaps it helps to look at how Paul started his second letter to the Corinthians, emoting about how in Asia, he and Timothy "were burdened excessively, beyond our strength, so that we despaired even of life."[5]

The good news is that you don't have to be like either Paul or Peter. You get to be an individual. You get to have your own experiences, make your own mistakes, enjoy your own successes, and even suffer your own consequences. The fact that both Peter and Paul share in the glory of Christ's overwhelming victory, no matter how they fared emotionally or endured physically on this earth, should be a comfort to us all.

THE FACT THAT BOTH PETER AND PAUL SHARE IN THE GLORY OF CHRIST'S OVERWHELMING VICTORY, NO MATTER HOW THEY FARED EMOTIONALLY OR ENDURED PHYSICALLY ON THIS EARTH, SHOULD BE A COMFORT TO US ALL.

Paul gives us a key to how to overcome in the midst of despair:

"Indeed, we had the sentence of
death within ourselves so that we would not
trust in ourselves, but in God who raises the dead,
*who rescued us from so great a **danger of death**, and*
will rescue us, He on whom we have set our hope."[6]

Paul fixed his mind on the knowledge that, amid all of the dangers and persecution he faced, he had already died with Christ. Therefore he had already been assured of his participation in Christ's resurrection.

It was *He on whom we have set our hope* that was the central figure of assurance.

Paul could thus write to the Church in Rome:

> *"... we also celebrate in our tribulations, knowing*
> *that tribulation brings about perseverance; and*
> *perseverance, proven character; and proven character,*
> *hope; and hope does not disappoint, because the*
> *love of God has been poured out within our hearts*
> *through the Holy Spirit who was given to us."[7]*

Once again, God is central to overcoming tribulation. In fact, with His love in our hearts, we can celebrate our tribulations. I suspect, however, that Paul did more celebrating *after* the tribulations and *after* the despair.

It is a rare moment when we respond as the disciples did after being flogged at the order of the Sanhedrin and ordered not to preach in the name of Jesus:

> *"So they went on their way from the presence of*
> *the Council, rejoicing that they had been considered*
> *worthy to suffer shame for His name."[8]*

THIRST

Perhaps the reason we suffer burnout is because we overwork ourselves. It may be because we experience disappointment, betrayal, and rejection. Or, it could be that we fell short of our own expectations. No matter the reason we reached the end of ourselves, and regardless of vain comparisons to the Lord's apostles, one thing—the best thing—that we can work on is adjusting our sense of thirst.

If we are honest, we have sought too much from the affirmations of man. We have created expectations of large, bustling ministries. We have imagined excitement in our services, acceptance from even the most hardened unbeliever, and fruit from our ministries that enrich our immediate needs. If we let ourselves see it, it is quite possible that we have been living for stolen water and bread eaten in secret.[9]

Our soul appetites—the things for which we hunger and thirst in our innermost being—have not suffered the cross. Dietrich Bonhoeffer famously wrote, "When Christ calls a man, He bids him come and die."[10] This quote recalls the words of Jesus:

> *"And He was saying to them all, 'If anyone*
> *wants to come after Me, he must deny himself,*
> *take up his cross daily, and follow Me.'"[11]*

We believe we died when we prayed the sinners' prayer, or when we were baptized, or when we realized the call to ministry.

But did you die?

I recently saw this saying printed on a shirt. It was intended to mock people who complained about their muscle pain the day after a hard workout. I read it as a question about whether I have ever truly died to myself completely. My appetites often give me away. I am not as willing to do everything my Lord asks of me as I thought I might be at this point in my life. I like certain comforts, and I like to bargain with God that I will do His will *if* I can keep some of them.

I enjoy fasting, but I am not very good at it. I have had some truly amazing spiritual growth during and after fasts. I have had prayers answered. But most of the time, my three-day fast becomes a one-day fast with two days of compromises. My juice fasts end up including coffee and sodas. (Coffee *is* from the juice of a bean, so there's that.) My

Daniel fasts include cheats, like corn chips and salsa. I hunger and thirst after many things to which I have not yet died.

Those fasts have helped reset my tastes, though. The Daniel Fast, a 10- or 14- or 21-day fast (your choice) that is essentially vegan, takes a bit to get used to. However, once you are off sugar and fast food for a week or so, *real food* starts to regain its flavor. Orange juice is incredibly sweet and delicious. Spices and herbs make a bigger impact in smaller quantities. I am always surprised at how good fruits and vegetables taste when I'm not eating lab-created, chemically treated foods.

COULD IT BE THAT WHEN I AM PREOCCUPIED WITH THINGS OF THIS WORLD, I AM LESS ABLE TO TASTE THE GOODNESS OF GOD?

Once I die to the carnal dietary intake, the truly *good* things regain their flavor. Could it be that when I am preoccupied with things of this world, I am less able to taste the goodness of God? When I am focused on productivity, success, wealth, fame, activity, and entertainment, am I truly able to "taste and see that the Lord is good?"[12] If I were to reassess what my values are, how many are proved by my actions? How do I show my appetites by how I live my life?

The most pertinent question I go over regarding my own burnout experience is this:

- How much of my burnout was due to a thirst for all the wrong things?

And a question parallel to and more painful than that one:

- Does my soul thirst for God the way a deer pants for the water brooks?

I know I have not guarded my time with God, my worship, my Bible study, my fasting, or any other spiritual disciplines in such a way that I could say that my thirst is always for the Spirit. I have yet to meet anyone—a pastor or not—who has perfectly followed their thirst for God alone. What would it look like if we did just that?

HIDDEN WITH CHRIST

"For you have died, and your life is
hidden with Christ in God."[13]

Taking up our crosses daily means dying daily to ourselves. However, upon dying, we find our lives *"hidden with Christ in God."* Ponder that for a moment. What can touch us in that place?

Nothing.

Disappointment cannot.

Fear cannot.

Shame cannot.

Burnout cannot.

This is a mystery.

What does it look like to be *"hidden with Christ in God"*?

I believe it is a matter of identity. Jesus walked daily in perfect harmony with His identity. His integrity was unimpeachable, unshakeable. He was the same person before sinners and fishermen as in front of Pharisees and governors. He was not a respecter of persons. He knew fully who He was and what exactly was His mission on earth. And yet it was a daily acknowledgment—not a storehouse, but a cupboard. His acceptance of human limitations made Jesus daily dependent upon His Heavenly Father.

Our identity—the core of who we are and what we were created to do—is hidden with Christ in God. However, we can only discover it when He bids us come … and we die. The life of every Christian is about discovering that identity. How can we, leaders of His Church, preach and teach such a thing if we do not daily exhibit utter reliance upon our Father in Heaven? How can we expect others to get that lesson if we do not express it in our lives? I have perhaps learned more about that from godly people in my life that were not clergy than I have from pastors.

When we become aware of our identity in Him, we become intrepid, unmovable, focused, and alert. We are not caught off-guard. We have proper expectations of our ministries. We don't look to those to whom we minister for validation. We don't seek the limelight. We don't worry about what tomorrow will bring, how we will be clothed, or what we will eat. We know that God will provide all that we need for all that He has called us to do.

I weigh these truths daily nowadays. When I feel the pressures of where I must be next, I capture myself in this day and try to give God tomorrow. When I sense that someone needs ministry from me, I don't assume that I was preordained to be their answer, just the servant who points them to the One who *is* the answer. I have reset my expectations upon miracles, signs, and wonders according to His good pleasure. I know that most healing is a process, not a destination. Most of all, I have started to know the good Father, not the slave master, but the patient, loving *Abba* who sees me as His beloved child.

WHEN I FEEL THE PRESSURES OF WHERE I MUST BE NEXT, I CAPTURE MYSELF IN THIS DAY AND TRY TO GIVE GOD TOMORROW.

Well, I am at least in the process of attaining to those things. I still lose sight of them quite easily. However, I know my thirst is changing as I focus more and more on God. Having suffered from burnout, I know it does not define me. Consider His names:

- He is *Jehovah Rapha*, God my healer.

- He is *Jehovah Jireh,* the Lord will provide.

- He is *Jehovah M'Koddishkem,* the Lord who sanctifies.

- He is *Jehovah Nissi*, the Lord, my victory.

- He is *Jehovah Elyon,* the Lord, most high.

- He is *Jehovah Raah,* the Lord, my shepherd.

- He is *Jehovah Sabaoth,* the Lord of Hosts.

- He is *Jehovah Shalom,* the Lord of peace.

- He is *Jehovah Shammah,* the Lord is present.

- He is *Jehovah Hoseenu,* the Lord, our maker.

- He is *Jehovah Tsidkenu,* the Lord, our righteousness.

The list goes on. When I find myself in Him, I find myself surrounded, protected, filled, provided for, and at peace. My end will be better than my beginning or my present. I am bound for eternity in Him, in glory. My identity is fixed in Him. Why look elsewhere?

Sin was not necessary, but it was inevitable. Burnout is not necessary, but neither is it inevitable. Justification is both necessary and inevitable. So is sanctification, glorification, and habitation. All things, both necessary and inevitable, are found in Him. My life is hidden with Christ in God, so I have all the necessary and inevitable things. Why do I wrestle with those things which are neither necessary nor inevitable?

***Blessed are those who hunger and thirst for
righteousness, for they will be satisfied.***[14]

You joined ministry–His ministry–with a hunger and a thirst for His righteousness. I don't doubt that. You have studied, learned, watched, listened, and put your hand to the plow. Then it became real. If you admit it, your sights may never have been fixed on Christ as fully as they should have been. However, the single most important thing you can do to be effective from here on out is to sharpen your focus on Jesus. This is not just a call to more Bible study but to concerted worship and attentive prayer. It is the only way to get off the treadmill and feel the freedom of the pastureland.

Satisfaction is not found in crowds cheering, books selling, getting "likes" or "follows," or even in the new iPhone. Satisfaction is found in hearing these words:

*"Well done, good and faithful servant. You have been faithful
over a little; I will set you over much. Enter into the joy of your
master."*[15]

Satisfaction is found in being faithful over what you have been given, even if it was less than the church next to you; even if it resulted in betrayal; even if it meant you weren't as effective as you thought you should be. Satisfaction is found in His voice, not in man's.

As I close this book, I examine my past and present motives. I have not always been a "good and faithful servant." I have been often, though. And I am learning. But it never was about my goodness and faithfulness to begin with; it was about His goodness and His faithfulness. As much as my ministry is about reaching others, it is still also about Him reaching me when I could not reach Him.

He has made me His righteousness—clothed me with it, and imputed it to me.

In the final analysis, it has not been my ministry, my life, or my deeds that have pleased Him. He was pleased to make me like Jesus, and I am, as you are, still a work in progress. All that He has done or will do through me is to His glory. When I rest in that truth, I find myself in Him.

REFLECTION

"For now we see in a mirror dimly, but then face
to face; now I know in part, but then I will know
fully, just as I also have been fully known."
1 CORINTHIANS 13:12

The only reflection left is how you go forth and reflect Him. Let your future in ministry be as accurate a reflection of Jesus as you are able. Take the time to know Him and be found in Him, then go, fulfill the Great Commission in the way He has uniquely fitted you to do it.

PRAYER OF ENCOURAGEMENT

Father, I am convicted and convinced. I kneel before You with a renewed sense of my calling—Your drawing—and the flicker of first love's flame rekindled in my heart. Help me to abide in You, in all things to be found in You, to dwell in the pastureland, and to reject the treadmill, however familiar or noble or even spiritual it may seem.

I choose my relationship with You over my desire to do good things in Your name or to be recognized for my service.

I wish only to bring You more glory and to rest in the surety of Your great love and Your great care for me. Help me comprehend what it is to be fully known by You—my motives, my misgivings, my failures—and yet fully loved by You. Make me more like Jesus, and fill my heart with peace. In Christ Jesus, I pray, amen.

ENDNOTES

1   John 4:14.

2   Diane J. Chandler, "Pastoral Burnout and the Impact of Personal Spiritual Renewal, Rest-Taking, and Support System Practices," *Pastoral Psychology* 58, no. 3 (06, 2009): 284.

3   2 Corinthians 11:21b-27.

4   2 Corinthians 11:28-29a.

5   2 Corinthians 1:8b.

6   2 Corinthians 1:9-10a.

7   Romans 5:3-5.

8   Acts 5:41.

9   See Proverbs 9:17.

10   Dietrich Bonhoeffer, *The Cost of Discipleship* (London: SCM Press, 1948, 2001), 44.

11   Luke 9:23.

12   Psalm 34:8; Hebrews 6:5; 1 Peter 2:3.

13   Colossians 3:3.

14   Matthew 5:6.

15   Matthew 25:21, ESV.

ANALYSIS

O n that pages that follow, I share question-by-question graphs showing participant responses by percentage of participants. Twenty-seven participants gave their responses on the Francis Burnout Inventory, both before and after the study.

You can see that the overall trend was a positive change in burnout rates among the participants (indicating relief) after raising burnout awareness and creating better connections between participants and their sending sources.

To review the full study, see *First Responder Chaplaincy: Sending Sources as Key Social Support Structures* found at:

https://digitalcommons.liberty.edu/doctoral/3202/

I feel drained in fulfilling my ministry roles

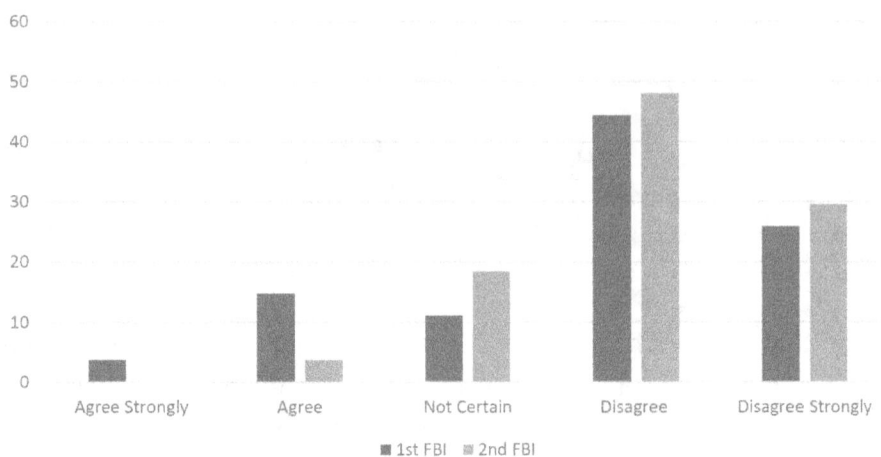

Fatigue and irritation are part of my daily experience

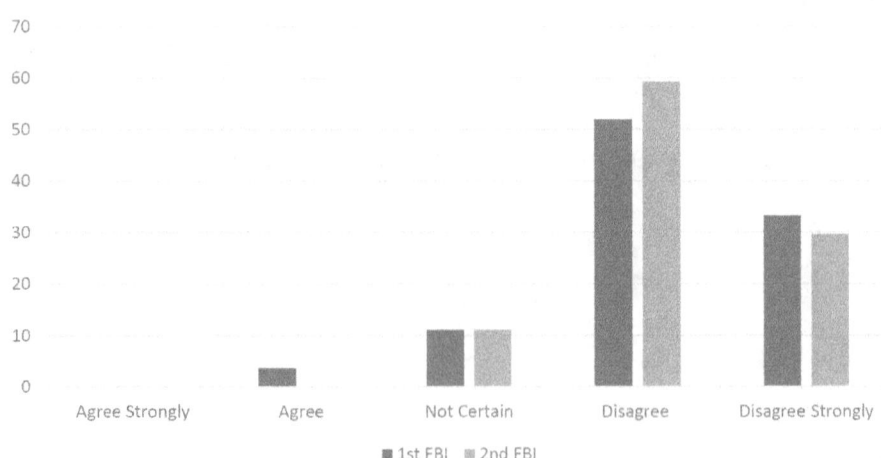

I am invaded by sadness I can't explain

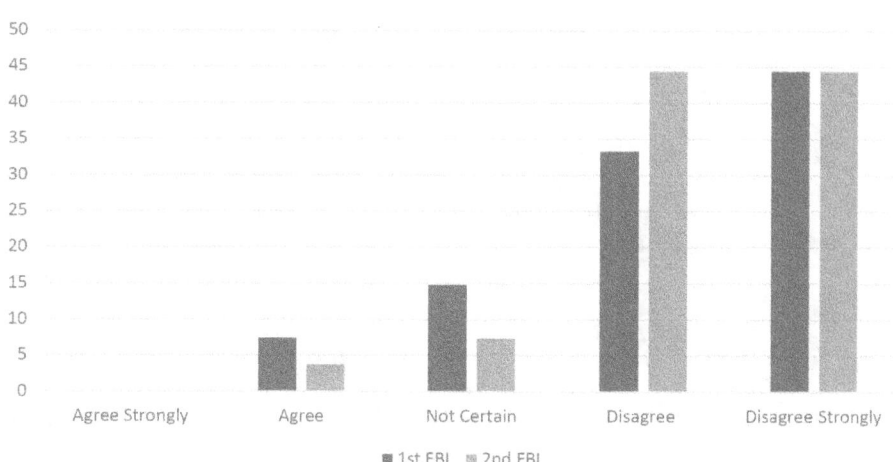

I am feeling negative or cynical about the people with whom I work

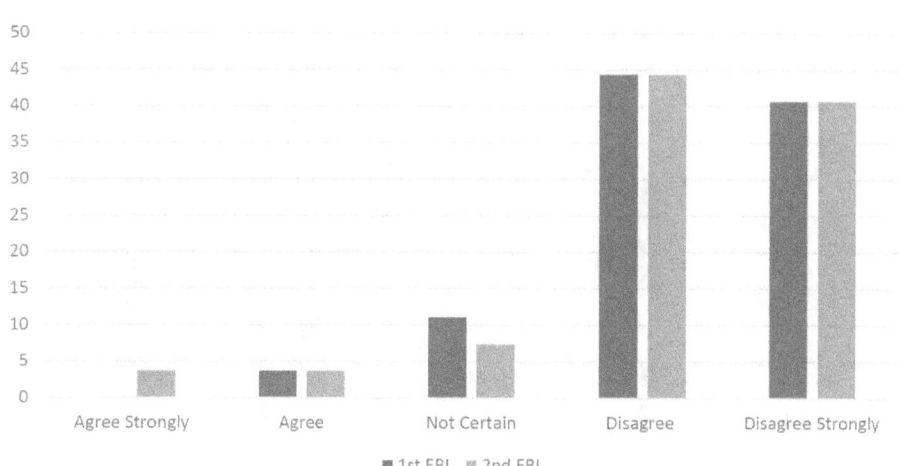

I always have enthusiasm for my work

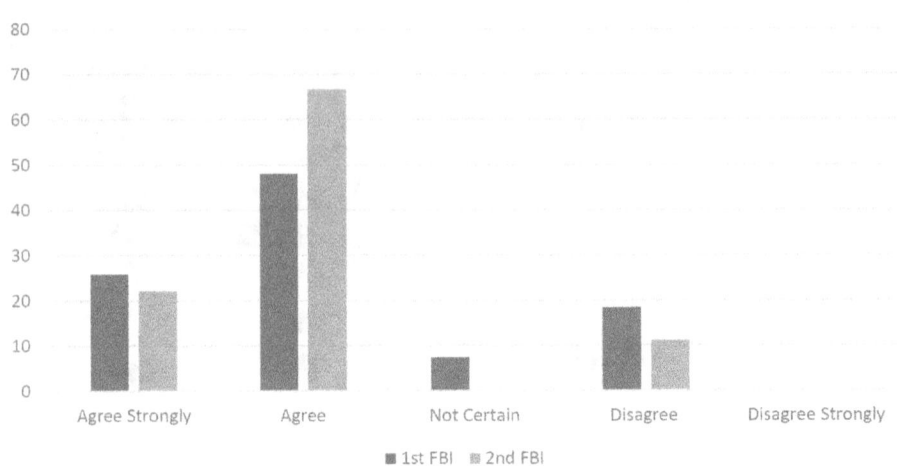

My humor has a cynical or biting tone

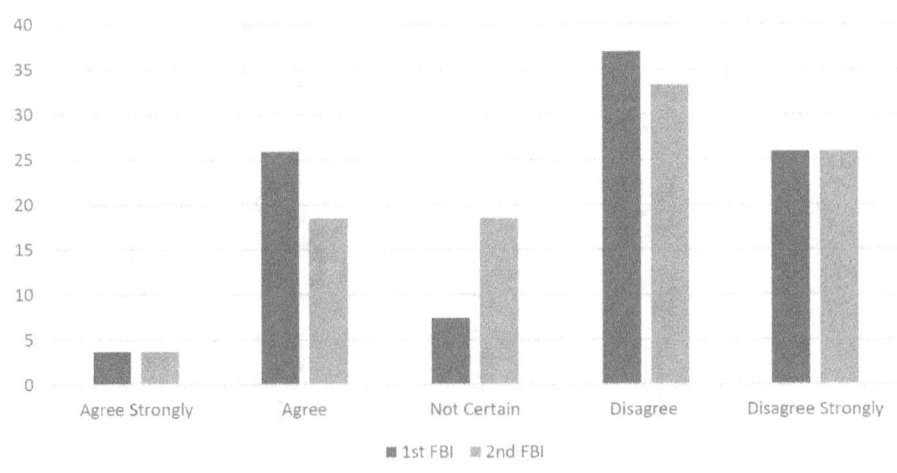

I find myself spending less and less time with those among whom I minister

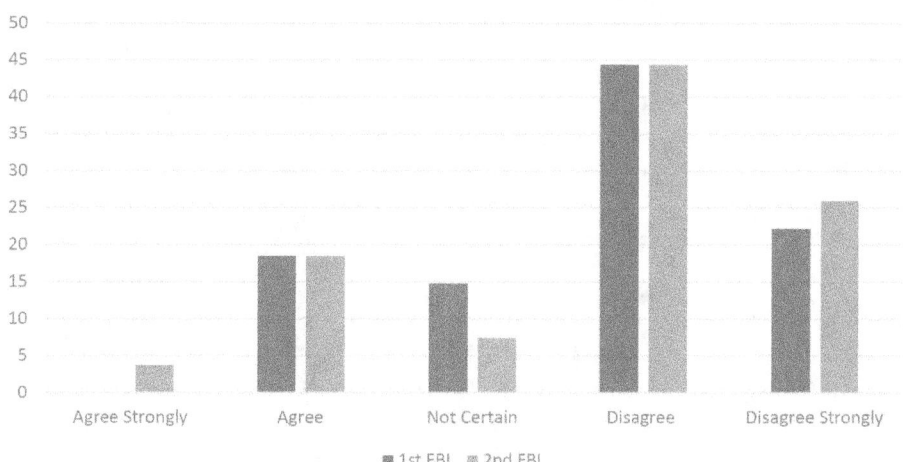

I have been discouraged by the lack of support for me here

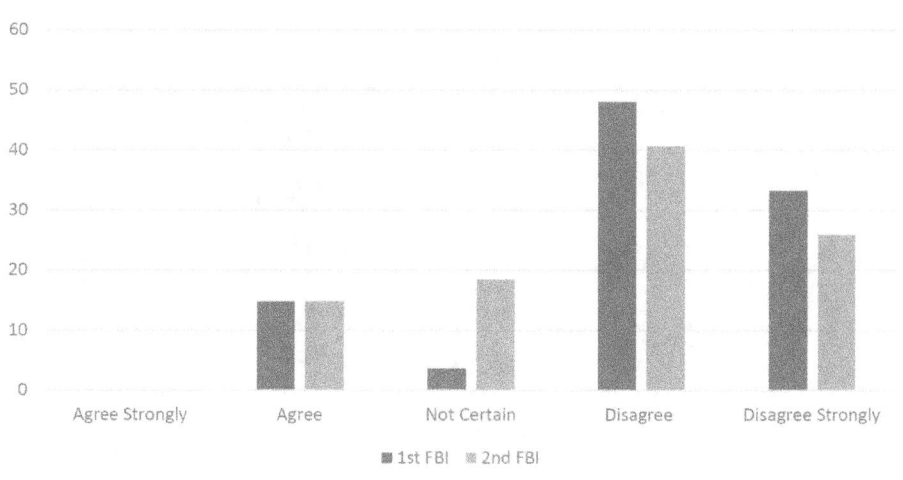

I find myself frustrated in my attempts to accomplish tasks important to me

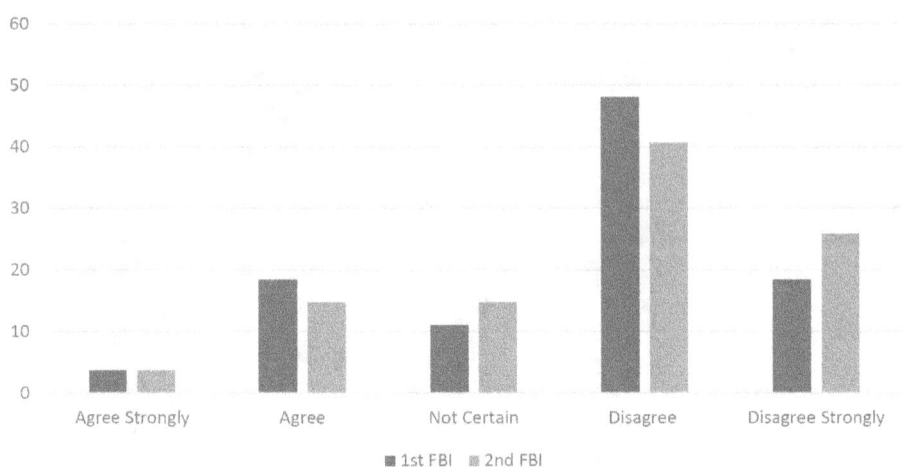

I am less patient with those among whom I minister than I used to be

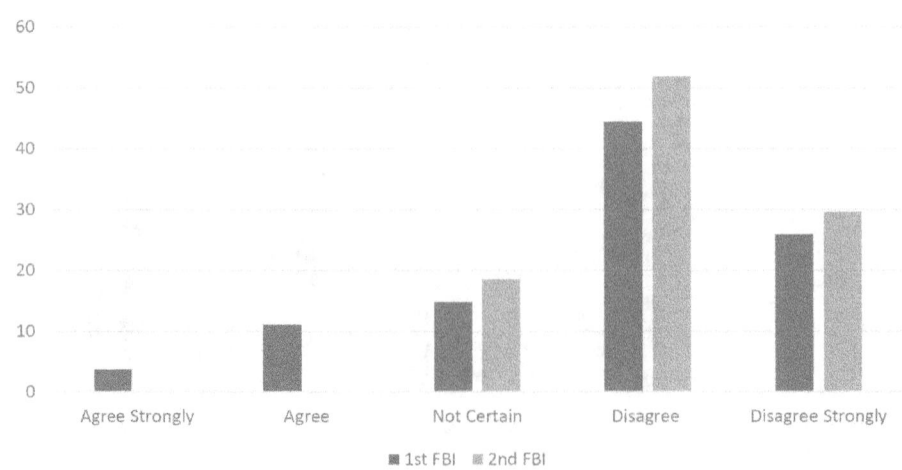

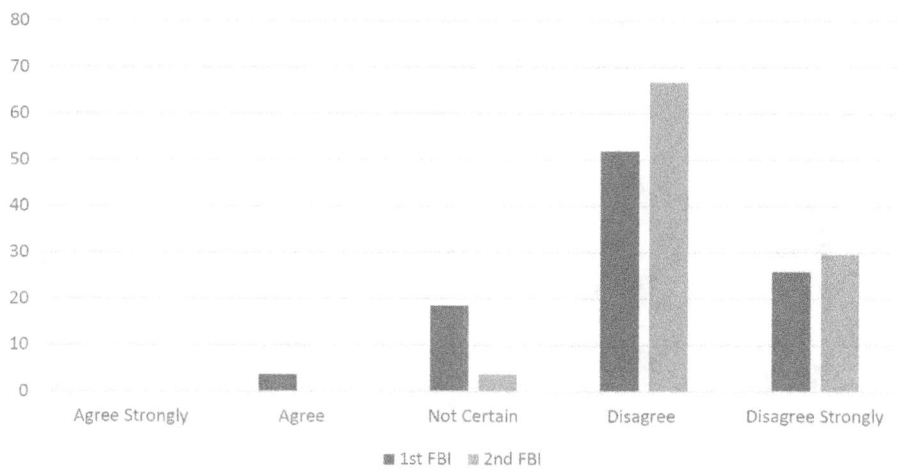

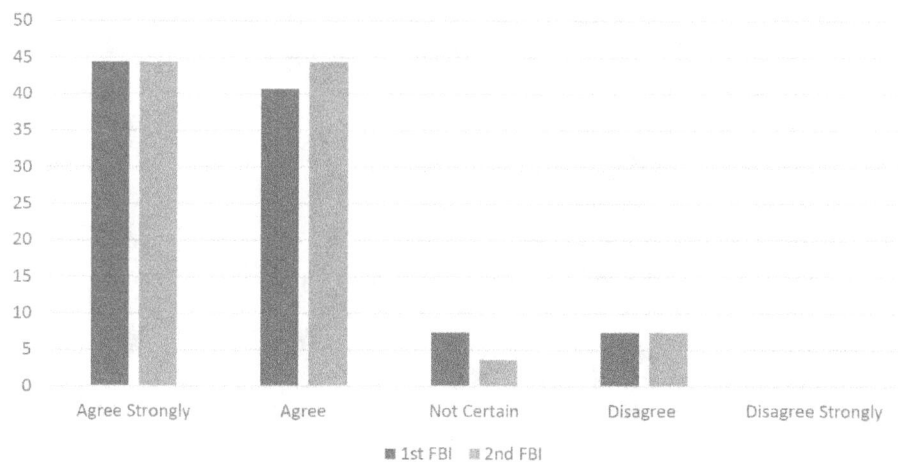

I gain a lot of personal satisfaction from working with people in my current ministry

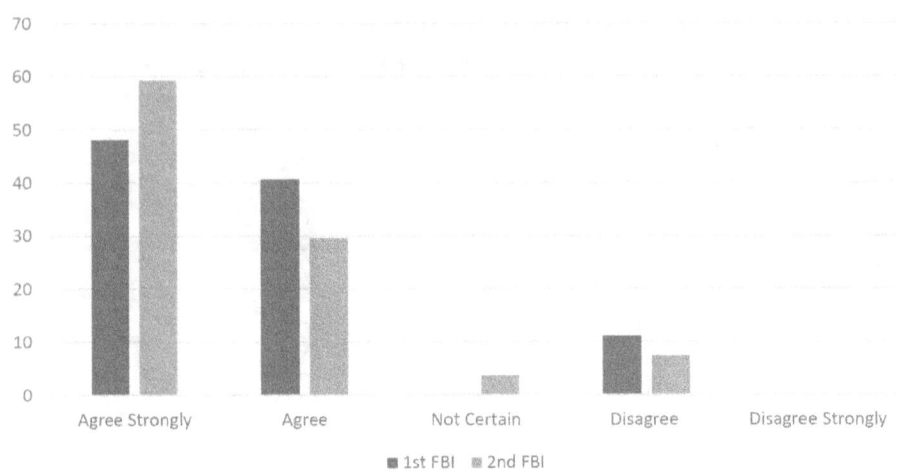

I deal very effectively with the problems of people in my current ministry

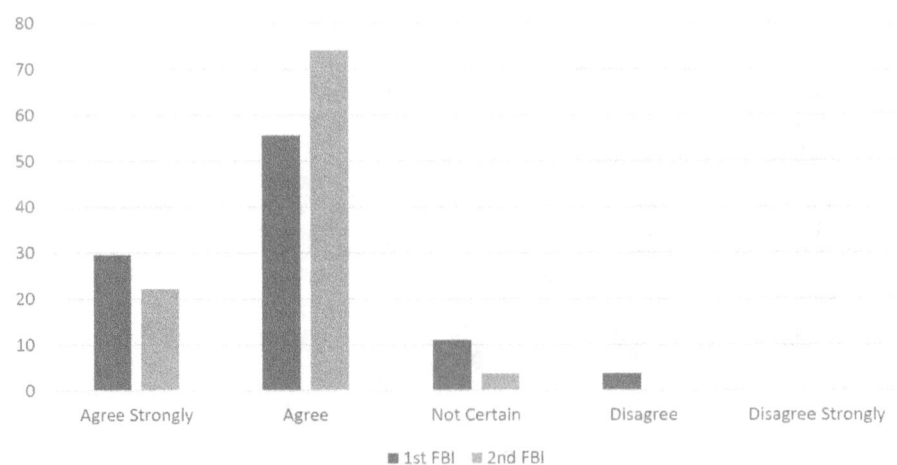

I can easily understand how those among whom I minister feel about things

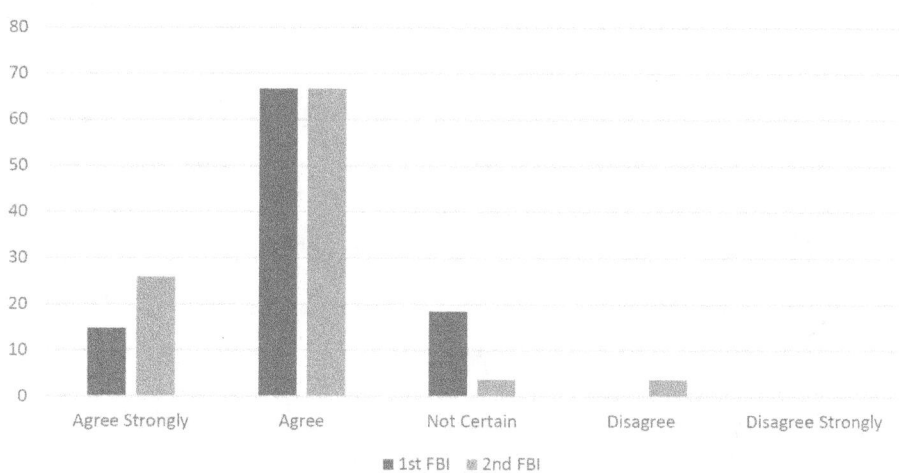

I feel very positive about my current ministry

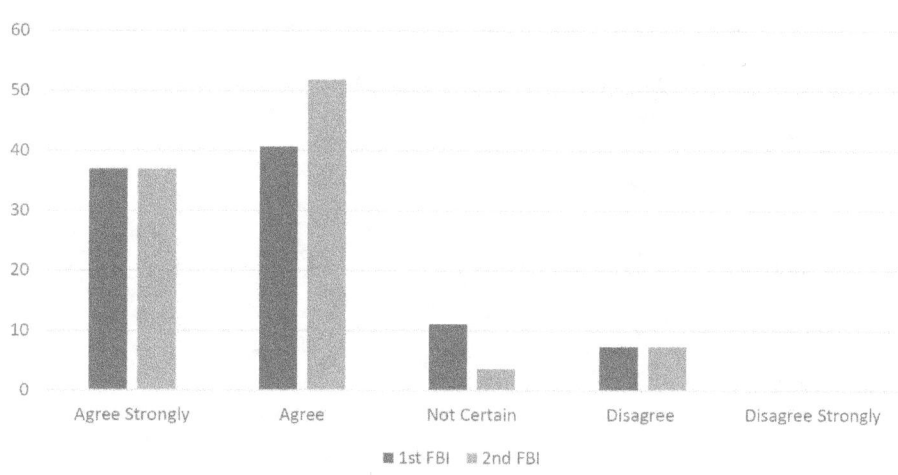

I feel that my chaplain ministry has a positive influence on people's lives

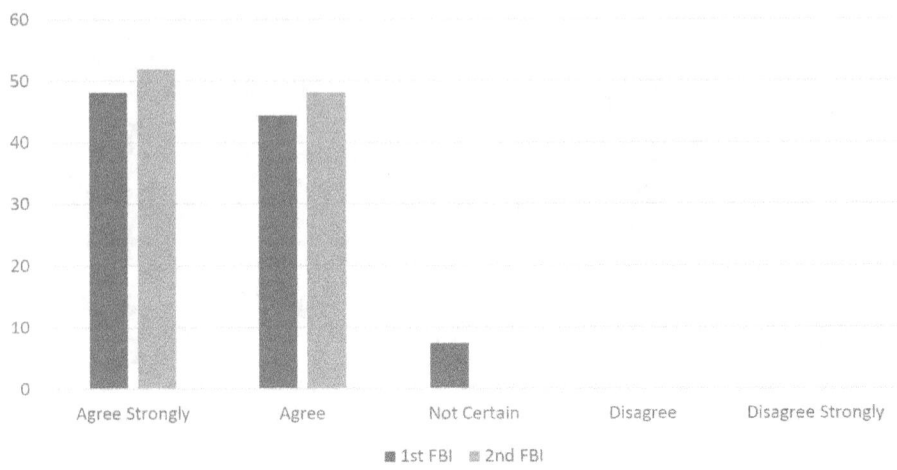

I feel that my chaplain ministry has a positive influence on people's faith

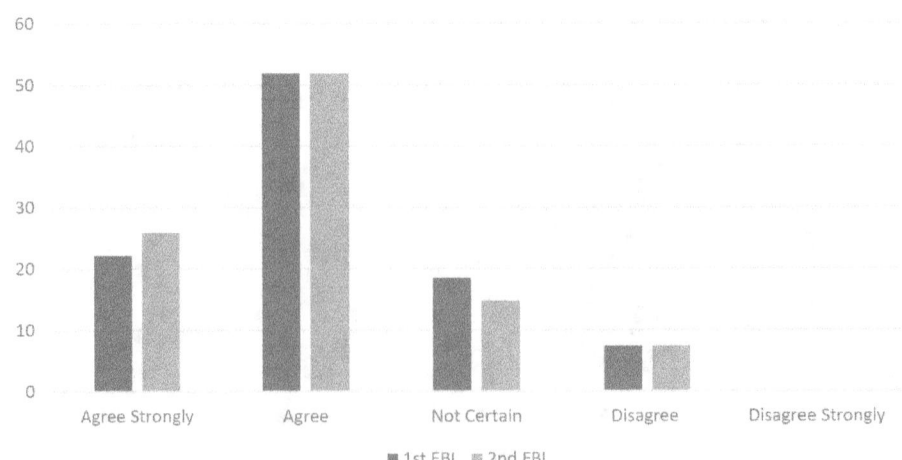

I feel my ministry is really appreciated by people

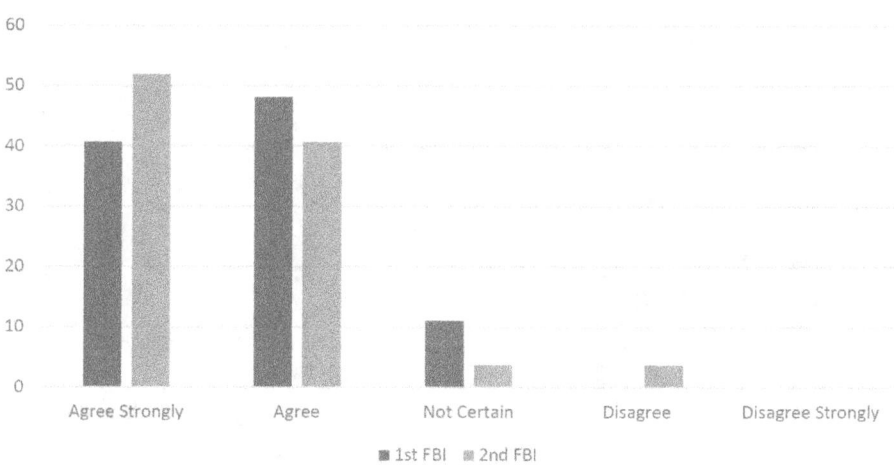

I am really glad I entered the ministry

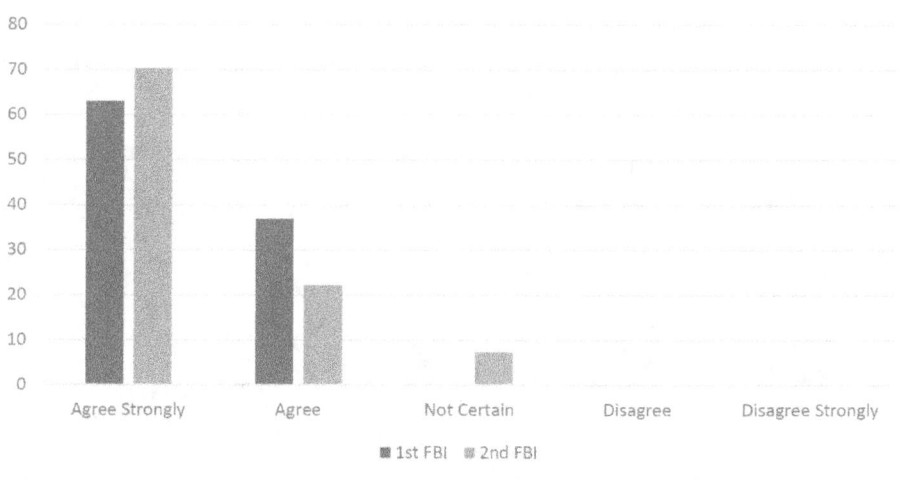

The ministry here gives real purpose and meaning to my life

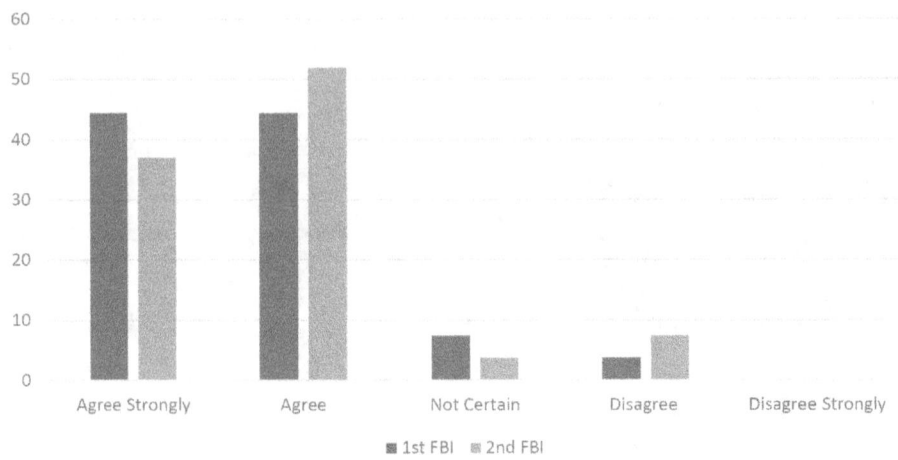

I gain a lot of personal satisfaction from fulfilling my ministry roles

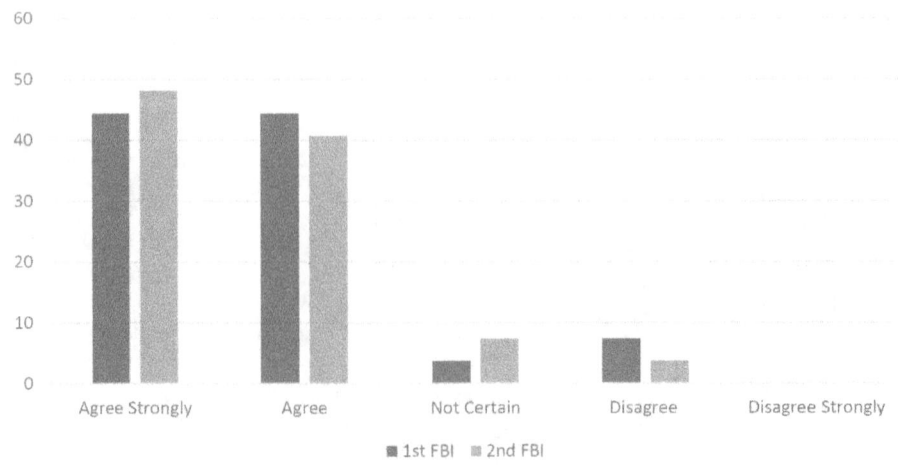

STATISTICAL ANALYSIS OF THE FBI

The following is a statistical analysis of the FBI and other elements of the study I promised in Chapter 3. I owe a great debt of gratitude to Dr. Corey Cook, Associate Professor of Psychology at Pacific Lutheran University, for providing a behavioral sciences analysis of the data.

BASELINE FBI

The Francis Burnout Inventory (FBI) was the quantitative measure of burnout taken by all twenty-seven First Responder Chaplains (FRCs) participating in this study. The FRCs took an initial FBI to establish a baseline response in Phase 1, then followed up with a final FBI iteration in Phase 3 to assess the impact of the intervention against their perceptions of Emotional Exhaustion and Personal Accomplishment.

- The average age of participants was 60.96, with a standard deviation of 11.22.

- The average years in FR ministry was 8.31.

- Internal reliability scores were divided between the two effects assessed by the FBI (EE=Emotional Exhaustion and PA=Personal Accomplishment).

- The responses to the eleven-question Scale of Emotional Exhaustion in Ministry showed good reliability with an alpha of .887.

- Responses to the eleven-question Satisfaction in Ministry Scale showed strong reliability with an alpha of .909.

- The eleven items from each scale were averaged into one score.

- Item 5, "I am invaded by sadness I can't explain," was reverse-coded for consistency.

- A paired-samples t-test revealed an overall sample report of higher levels of Personal Accomplishment (M = 4.21, SD = 0.57) than Emotional Exhaustion (M = 2.26, SD = 0.59).

- A strong inverse correlation exists, however, between EE (M = 2.26, SD = 0.59) and PA (M = 4.21, SD = .057), r (27) = -.72, p <.001.

- In other words, as PA scores increase, EE scores tend to decrease. This result stands contrary to the balanced affect theory of the FBI — namely, that individuals in ministry can, and often do, experience high levels of a negative effect (Emotional Exhaustion) while still maintaining high levels of a positive effect (sense of Personal Accomplishment).

- Notably, the sample of twenty-seven chaplains in this study may well be too small to conclude that First Responder Chaplaincy differs with the balanced effect found repeatedly to exhibit a balanced effect in pulpit ministry. (Note: The study addresses this further in Chapter 5.)

CORRELATIONS TO THE EFFECT OF SUPPORT ON EMOTIONAL EXHAUSTION AND SATISFACTION IN MINISTRY

To assess the correlation between support and exhaustion and support and satisfaction, FBI scores for Survey of Emotional Exhaustion in Ministry (SEEM) and Satisfaction in Ministry Survey (SIMS) were compared with a demographic question, "My sending source provides me _____ support."

- Possible answers were "No," "Some," "Much," and "I have no sending source."

- Answers were re-coded onto a "1 = no support/no source" to "4 = much support" scale (M=2.83, SD = 1.19).

- Twenty-three of twenty-seven answers were valid for the analysis, while four answers were essentially non-responsive.

- This iteration of the FBI revealed sending source support and exhaustion, r (23) = -.21, p = .33, and sending source support and satisfaction, r (23) = .17, p = .43, offering no correlation between sending source support and either EE or PA.

CORRELATIONS TO AGE

The author tested the correlation between age and levels of exhaustion and satisfaction, drawing from responses to both the Questionnaire and the FBI.

- Older respondents tended to report significantly reduced levels of EE, r (27) = -.38, p = .05.

- There was, however, no correlation between age and PA, r (27) = .24, p = .23. This is an interesting result, as the age skews toward the higher end.

- Sixteen of the twenty-seven participants ranged in age from 60-83, seven participants were in their 50s, and four were under 50. The youngest participant was 33 years of age, while the next three eldest in the under 50 category were 43, 44, and 49.

FINAL FBI

The same twenty-seven FRC participants took the final iteration of the FBI approximately 3.5 to 4 months after the initial baseline iteration. Intervening study-related events included an interview conducted by the investigator with each of the twenty-seven FRC participants, meetings between the investigator and eleven FRCs with their sending sources, and a Solutions Focus Group in which five FRCs participated.

- With Item 5 reverse coded as before, Emotional Exhaustion (EE) responses showed good reliability with a .860 score.

- The eleven questions in the Survey of Emotional Exhaustion in Ministry (SEEM) were averaged into one score, M = 2.02 and SD = 0.59.

- Responses on the Satisfaction In Ministry Survey (SIMS) showed strong reliability with a score of .934.

- The eleven questions indicating Personal Accomplishment (PA) were also averaged into one score, with M = 4.29 and SD = 0.58.

- The paired-samples t-test for the sample of twenty-seven FRCs reported higher levels of PA (M=4.29, SD = 0.58) than EE (M= 2.02, SD = 0.59), t (26) = 11.02, p < .001.

- The FBI indicated a strong inverse correlation between exhaustion and satisfaction, r (27) = -.685, p < .001.

- The indication is that as the FRC experiences increased levels of exhaustion, they become less satisfied in their sense of accomplishment.

SELF-ASSESSMENT OF MINISTRY BURNOUT

A self-assessment question, separate from the FBI, queried the participants, "I am presently experiencing burnout in my chaplaincy ministry."

- Responses included: "To a great extent," "To some extent," "To a small extent," and "Not at all."

- The responses were scale-coded 0 to 3, with 0 indicating "Not at all" (M = .40, SD = .645).

- This self-assessment revealed a negative correlation with PA, r (25) = -.645, p <.001, and a positive correlation with exhaustion, r (27) = .667, p <.001.

- This finding indicates that those who express lower PA and higher EE tended to perceive themselves as experiencing burnout in their ministry.

FINAL FBI SCORES COMPARED TO BASELINE FBI SCORES

A paired-sample t-test was conducted to compare FRC baseline FBI scores with their final iteration scores.

- Supporting Hypothesis 4, the comparison showed a significant decrease in reported EE, t (26) = 3.25, p = .003.

- However, the results relating to PA revealed slightly higher scores, though of insignificant value, between baseline and final iterations, t (26) = -1.15, p = .26.

- A possible explanation for this is a ceiling effect of high PA scores indicated in the baseline FBI report.

MEET THE AUTHOR

CHRISTOPHER A. BASSET, D.MIN.

Chris is a retired Pastor of 25 years. He is a retired Chaplain with 33 years of military service, including deployments to Iraq and Afghanistan. He spent ten years as a Police Chaplain with his city police department and served 15 years as a Sheriff's Deputy, Detective, and Master Police Officer.

Chris received his Master of Divinity Degree from Fuller Theological Seminary and his Doctor of Ministry Degree from Liberty University. He recently published a study on First Responder Chaplains and Burnout, and he is a master trainer in suicide intervention.

Chris enjoys RV life and serving the RV community as a chaplain. He loves running, weightlifting, Taekwondo, teaching Bible studies, enjoying the beach, and dating his beautiful wife, Cheri. Together they have four adult children and one grandchild.

Passionate about supporting missions, he travels regularly to Tanzania to teach at a school for pastors. He is dedicated to writing and speaking and is available for church or conference speaking engagements or as a radio, webcast, or podcast guest. He can speak with authority on a wide range of topics from his background and experience, but these topics are his specialty:

- Ministry Burnout Avoidance and Recovery
- 4th Dimensional Faith
- Suicide Intervention and the spirit of Suicide
- Our Identity in Christ

To learn more or invite Chris, visit:
www.4thDimensionMinistries.org

INTERESTED IN BECOMING OR GROWING AS A CHAPLAIN?

Chaplains of all ministry sectors seeking Continuing Education credits can take courses online with Chris and other instructors at:

www.ChaplainTrainingAcademy.org